W9-BMR-666

OXIDATION AND REDUCTION

Grolier Educational
SHERMAN TURNPIKE, DANBURY, CONNECTICUT 06816

First published in the United States in 1998
by Grolier Educational, Sherman Turnpike,
Danbury, CT 06816

Author
Brian Knapp, BSc, PhD
Project consultant
*Keith B. Walshaw, MA, BSc, DPhil
(Head of Chemistry, Leighton Park School)*
Project Director
Duncan McCrae, BSc
Editor
Mary Sanders, BSc
Special photography
Ian Gledhill
Illustrations
The Ascenders Partnership, David Woodroffe
Electronic page makeup
The Ascenders Partnership
Designed and produced by
EARTHSCAPE EDITIONS
Print consultants
Chromo Litho Ltd
Reproduced in Malaysia by
Global Colour
Printed and bound in Italy by
L.E.G.O. SpA

Library of Congress Cataloging-in-Publication Data
ChemLab
  p. cm.
  Includes indexes.
  Contents: v.1.Gases, liquids, and solids –
v.2.Elements, compounds, and mixtures – v.3.The
periodic table – v.4.Metals – v.5.Acids, bases, and salts
– v.6.Heat and combustion – v.7.Oxidation and
reduction – v.8.Air and water chemistry – v.9.Carbon
chemistry – v.10.Energy and chemical change –
v.11.Preparations – v.12. Tests.
ISBN 0-7172-9146-4 (set). – ISBN 0-7172-9153-7 (v.7).
  1. Chemistry – Juvenile literature. [1. Chemistry.]
I. Grolier Educational (Firm)
QD35.C52 1997
540-dc21   97-23250
                                                       CIP
                                                       AC

Picture credits
All photographs are from the **Earthscape
Editions** photolibrary except the following:
(c=center t=top b=bottom l=left r=right)
Copper Development Association 42br;
Mary Evans Picture Library 6tr, 7tr

*This product is manufactured from sustainable
managed forests. For every tree cut down at
least one more is planted.*

Contents

HOW TO USE THIS BOOK

These two pages show you how to get the most from this book.

❶ THE CONTENTS

Use the table of contents to see how this book is divided into themes. Each theme may have one or more demonstrations.

❷ THEMES

Each theme begins with a theory section on yellow-colored paper. Major themes may contain several pages of theory for the demonstrations that are presented on the subsequent pages. They also contain biographies of scientists whose work was important in the understanding of the theme.

❸ DEMONSTRATIONS

Demonstrations are at the heart of any chemistry study. However, many demonstrations cannot easily be shown to a whole class for health and safety reasons, because the demonstration requires a closeup view, because it is over too quickly, takes too long to complete, or because it requires special apparatus. The demonstrations shown here have been photographed especially to overcome these problems and give you a very closeup view of the key stages in each reaction.

The text, pictures, and diagrams are closely connected. To get the best from the demonstration, look closely at each picture as soon as its reference occurs in the text.

Many of the pictures show enlarged views of parts of the demonstration to help you see exactly what is happening. Notice, too, that most pictures form part of a sequence. You will find that it pays to look at the picture sequence more than once, and always be careful to make sure you can see exactly what is described in any picture before you move on.

The main heading for a demonstration or a set of demonstrations.

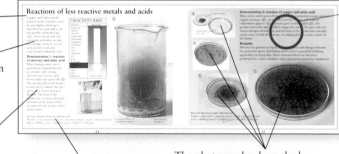

An introduction expands on the heading, summarizing the demonstration or group of demonstrations and their context in the theme.

Each demonstration is carefully explained and illustrated with photographs and, where necessary, with diagrams, tables, and graphs. The illustrations referred to are numbered ①, ②, ③, etc.

Chemical equations are shown where appropriate (see the explanation of equations at the bottom of page 5).

The photographs show the key stages that you might see if witnessing a demonstration firsthand. Examine them very carefully against the text description.

APPARATUS

The demonstrations have been carefully conducted as representative examples of the main chemical processes. The apparatus used is standard; but other choices are possible, and you may see different equipment in your laboratory. So make sure you understand the principles behind the apparatus selected. The key pieces of apparatus are defined in the glossary.

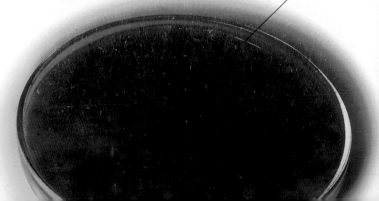

❹ GLOSSARY OF TECHNICAL TERMS

Words with which you may be unfamiliar are shown in small capitals where they first occur in the text. Use the glossary on pages 66–74 to find more information about these technical words. Over four hundred items are presented alphabetically.

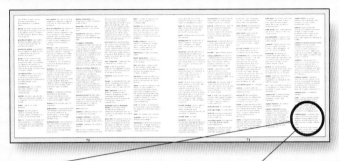

oxidizing agent: a substance that removes electrons from another substance being oxidized (and therefore is itself reduced) in a redox reaction. *Example:* chlorine (Cl_2).

❺ INDEX TO ALL VOLUMES IN THE SET

To look for key words in any of the 12 volumes that make up the ChemLab set, use the Master Index on pages 75 to 80. The instructions on page 75 show you how to cross-reference between volumes.

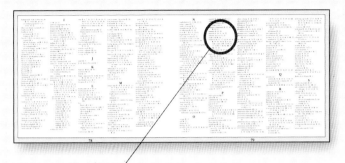

The most important locations of the term "oxidizing agent" are given in a master index that includes references to all of the volumes in the ChemLab set.

ABBREVIATIONS

Units are in the international metric system. Some units of measurement are abbreviated, or shortened, as follows:
°C = degrees Celsius
km = kilometer
m = meter
cm = centimeter
mm = millimeter
sq m = square meter
g = gram
kg = kilogram
kJ = kilojoule
l = liter

❻ CHEMICAL EQUATIONS

Important or relevant chemical equations are shown in written and symbolic form along with additional information.

What the reaction equation illustrates

Word equation

Symbol equation
The symbols for each element can be found in any Periodic Table.

Where relevant, the oxidation state is shown as Roman numerals in parentheses.

EQUATION: Reaction of copper and nitric acid

Copper + nitric acid ⟹ copper(II) nitrate + water + nitrogen dioxide

$Cu(s) + 4HNO_3(conc) ⟹ Cu(NO_3)_2(aq) + 2H_2O(l) + 2NO_2(g)$
Blue

The symbol indicating the state of each substance is shown as follows:
(*s*) = solid
(*g*) = gaseous
(*l*) = liquid
(*aq*) = aqueous
(*conc*) = concentrated

The two halves of the chemical equation are separated by the arrow that shows the progression of the reaction. Each side of the equation must balance.

Sometimes additional descriptions are given below the symbol equation.

The correct number of atoms, ions, and molecules and their proportions in any compound are shown by the numbers. A free electron is shown as an e⁻.

Introduction

The two opposite processes of REDUCTION and OXIDATION, often called redox reactions for short, (pronounced "reedocks") are among the most important and common chemical reactions.

Many of these redox reactions also have common names. For example, when something catches fire, it is oxidized in a redox reaction that is known as burning. CORROSION is another redox reaction, which, in the case of iron, we call rusting. Most of the processes used in industry to obtain metals from ores involve reduction in redox reactions, but these are known as refining. The electric current we obtain from a battery is a result of oxidation and reduction.

Many biological processes also involve oxidation and reduction. Plants use the energy of the Sun to make their tissues by reducing carbon dioxide from the air in a redox reaction called photosynthesis. In contrast, animals "burn" or oxidize food in a redox reaction called respiration. Similarly, the oxidation of fruit is a redox reaction that causes ripening or fermenting.

The history of our understanding of oxidation and reduction

The first group of reactions identified as being oxidation-reduction involved burning. Scientists tried to understand just how a substance changed as it burned. In 1697 Georg Stahl suggested that burning materials release "phlogiston," a fundamental but unseen part of all substances that would burn.

It took a century for an alternative view to be put forward. Antoine Lavoisier suggested that combustion is a chemical reaction in which a substance combines with oxygen gas from the air. Within a few years Karl Scheele, a Swedish chemist, and Joseph Priestley, an English chemist, had independently isolated oxygen from the air.

The use of the term oxidation (i.e., when there is the addition of oxygen to a substance) thus became the standard term for this kind of reaction. Similarly, it is defined that a reaction involves reduction if oxygen is lost (i.e., there is a reduction in the amount of oxygen in a substance).

In fact, as we shall see, oxygen is just one of several substances that can support burning and oxidize another substance, and so we have to be careful not to link oxidation simply with oxygen. Indeed, it was discovered in the 19th century that the processes of oxidation and reduction were not linked to the loss and gain of oxygen as ATOMS but were due to the loss or gain of ELECTRONS. This discovery provided the missing link between all of the substances that could support burning (for example, chlorine) and the way in which chemical cells (batteries) worked.

The more complete definition of an oxidation and reduction reaction is now based on the transfer of electrons. Redox is an important topic, since most reactions involve an exchange of electrons.

Antoine Laurent Lavoisier

Antoine Lavoisier (1743–1794) was born in Paris, France. As a result of his interest in chemistry, he was appointed to the National Gunpowder Commission, and his laboratory was in the Paris Arsenal.

Lavoisier has been called the "father of chemistry." Although the major classes of chemicals — acids, alkalis, salts, alkaline earths, and metals — had been defined, gases were poorly known and explained by the strange theory of a "fire-matter" called phlogiston. Lavoisier's main contribution was to begin to develop a logical theory to pull all these parts of chemistry together. His contributions to the need to make careful measurements were particularly valuable, and from this came the recognition that the weight of the reactants must equal the weight of the products of a reaction.

Lavoisier dispelled the phlogiston theory of combustion and replaced it with the theory of oxidation. The phlogiston theory said that combustible material such as coal or wood was rich in a material substance called phlogiston, named from a Greek word meaning "to set on fire." During combustion phlogiston was lost to the air. Metals were also said to be rich in phlogiston, which escaped slowly into the air, leaving behind a phlogiston-poor rust. The difference between combustion and rusting was simply in the speed with which phlogiston was lost: rapid transfer produced a flame, whereas a slow transfer caused rust. The problems with this theory included the fact that when a metal was roasted, it became heavier (whereas the loss of phlogiston should have made it lighter). This is what convinced Lavoisier that roasting caused air to combine with the metal, and he proved it by a series of careful experiments.

As soon as oxygen had been discovered, Lavoisier was able to prove that combustion was a chemical reaction in which oxygen combines with other elements.

Lavoisier was caught up in the French Revolution, and he was imprisoned and finally guillotined based on trumped-up charges. At the time, a fellow scientist remarked: "It took only an instant to cut off that head, and a hundred years may not produce another like it."

Oxidizing and reducing agents

Substances that cause oxidation are called oxidizing agents, while those that cause reduction are called reducing agents.

Some substances are better oxidizing agents than others. It all depends on how readily a substance takes up electrons. The most reactive nonmetals (see the Periodic Table below) are among the most effective oxidizing agents.

Because of its abundance in the atmosphere, oxygen gas (O_2) is by far the most common oxidizing agent. Ozone (O_3), another form of oxygen, is also an important oxidizing agent. Fluorine (F) is the strongest oxidizing agent of all the elements, and the other halogens — chlorine (Cl), bromine (Br), iodine (I) — are also powerful oxidizing agents.

There are also some strong reducing agents among the elements. Hydrogen (H_2) and the most reactive alkali metals in Groups 1 and 2 of the Periodic Table are among the most effective reducing agents. They include lithium (Li) and sodium (Na). Hydrogen was among the first elements to be recognized as a reducing agent. Because carbon (C) and sulfur (S) readily combine with oxygen (and will readily remove oxygen from compounds), they are also effective reducing agents, especially at high temperatures.

In this book you will find a wide variety of examples of redox reactions. Initially we will focus on the role of oxygen and hydrogen, then show how other gases can oxidize and reduce compounds, and how some substances are stronger reducing or oxidizing agents than others. Finally, we will see how redox tells us about the way metals react with one another, how corrosion works, and the fundamentals of electrochemical reactions.

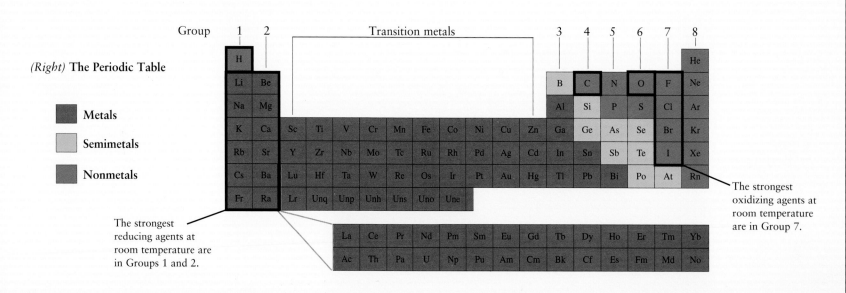

(Right) **The Periodic Table**

Metals

Semimetals

Nonmetals

The strongest reducing agents at room temperature are in Groups 1 and 2.

The strongest oxidizing agents at room temperature are in Group 7.

Oxidation in the atmosphere

Oxidation is an everyday phenomenon, especially on the streets of cities where pollution is common. The oxidation associated with the emission of nitrogen monoxide (also called nitric oxide) from vehicle exhausts can easily be demonstrated.

Demonstration: nitrogen monoxide and oxygen

Two gas jars are needed: the first is filled with nitrogen monoxide (NO, a colorless gas), and the other with oxygen (O_2, also a colorless gas) (①). When the gas jars are put together as shown in the pictures, and the separating glass cover slip pulled away (②), the nitrogen monoxide will mix with the oxygen and is oxidized to nitrogen dioxide (NO_2, a brown gas). Gas molecules are in constant motion, and so the contents of both gas jars soon become uniformly brown (③).

Remarks

Oxidation of exhaust gases in bright sunshine and calm air produces a brown haze called PHOTOCHEMICAL SMOG. Smog begins when gases are created in vehicle engines, where oxygen and nitrogen gas combine as the fuel burns to form nitrogen monoxide. When the gas passes out of the car exhaust, more oxygen is available from the atmosphere, and much of the nitrogen monoxide is oxidized to nitrogen dioxide.

EQUATION: Nitrogen monoxide reacting with oxygen
Nitrogen monoxide + oxygen ⇨ nitrogen dioxide
$2NO(g) ⇨ O_2(g) + 2NO_2(g)$

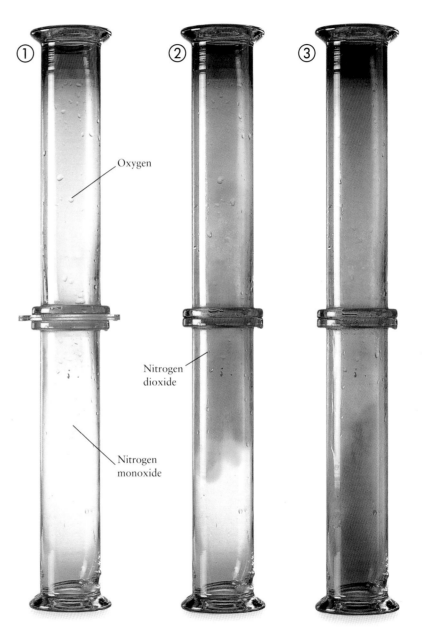

① ② ③

Oxygen

Nitrogen dioxide

Nitrogen monoxide

Oxidation and reduction of copper

Many reactions demonstrate that oxygen has been gained by a substance. This substance is said to have become oxidized, and the reaction is called oxidation. The substance that donated the oxygen is an example of an oxidizing agent. For example, copper and the oxidizing agent oxygen react to produce copper oxide.

In other reactions oxygen might be removed from a substance, for example, when hydrogen is passed over copper oxide. In this reaction copper oxide loses its oxygen and becomes copper metal. The copper oxide has been reduced to copper. The hydrogen is acting as a reducing agent.

The two demonstrations shown on the next six pages are designed to follow the progress of oxidation and reduction from copper metal through oxidation to copper oxide and then reduction back to copper metal again.

Demonstration 1: oxidation of copper

Some copper filings (shavings of fresh, clean copper) are placed in a ceramic dish. The ceramic dish is placed on a PIPE-CLAY TRIANGLE and a tripod, and heated strongly (①).

It takes only a couple of minutes for the copper filings to change from bright orange to a more brassy color and then to become progressively duller (②). Soon the copper becomes dark and finally turns black (③). As it does so, it changes to a powder. The copper has been oxidized to copper oxide.

EQUATION 1: Copper being oxidized by heating in air (oxygen)
copper + oxygen ⇨ *copper*(II) *oxide*
$2Cu(s) + O_2(g) \Rightarrow 2CuO(s)$

Demonstration 2: reduction of copper oxide

The copper oxide produced in the demonstration on page 10 has been formed through a reaction of copper with the oxygen of the air. To reduce the copper oxide back to copper again, a supply of hydrogen is used.

The copper oxide is transferred from the ceramic dish to a REDUCTION TUBE, which is a special form of boiling tube with a hole near the closed end (④). The copper oxide must be spread out so that its surface area is as large as possible. Next, a stopper and delivery tube are attached. The delivery tube is connected to a hydrogen supply.

A supply of hydrogen can be produced by reacting zinc and dilute hydrochloric acid (⑤). A continuous supply of hydrogen is needed, so the preparation must include sufficient reactants for a reaction lasting several minutes. To achieve this, a substantial quantity of zinc is placed in a conical flask, and the hydrochloric acid is dripped on to the zinc from a dropper funnel. Effervescence begins without heating. The delivery tube is now connected to the reduction tube so that hydrogen flows over the copper oxide and out of the hole at the far end. The copper oxide is heated strongly using a Bunsen flame (⑥).

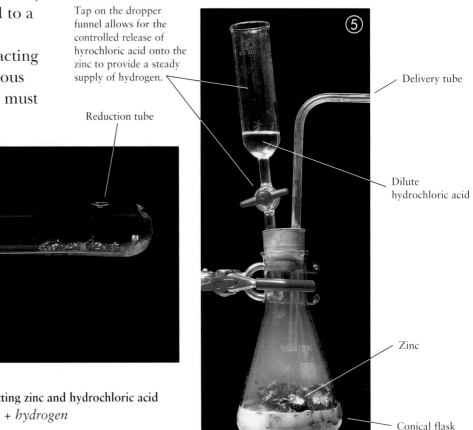

Tap on the dropper funnel allows for the controlled release of hyrochloric acid onto the zinc to provide a steady supply of hydrogen.

Reduction tube

Delivery tube

Dilute hydrochloric acid

Zinc

Conical flask

EQUATION 2: Production of hydrogen by reacting zinc and hydrochloric acid
Zinc + hydrochloric acid ⇨ zinc chloride + hydrogen
$Zn(s) + 2HCl(aq)$ ⇨ $ZnCl_2(aq) + H_2(g)$

When the hydrogen is flowing, excess hydrogen can be burned off by applying a flame to the hole in the reduction tube. The color of the flame varies from yellow (⑦) to green (⑧). The high temperature of the hydrogen flame tends to melt the glass around the hole, the sodium content of the glass coloring the flame yellow. From time to time tiny particles of the copper oxide powder are also caught up in the flow of hydrogen through the hole, and when they become hot, they show the characteristic green color of copper in the flame.

Within a few minutes the copper oxide begins to turn a dull red, then the red color become more reddish-pink as the last remains of the oxide are reduced. When the reduction is complete, the tube contains orange copper (⑨), the only net change being that the filings have been changed into copper powder.

Hydrogen is passed over the copper until cool; otherwise it will oxidize back to black copper oxide.

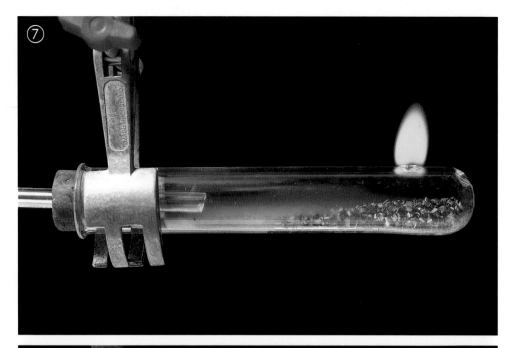

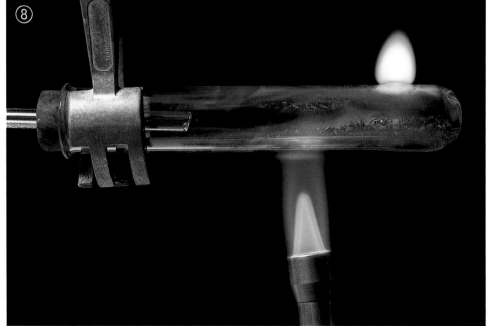

EQUATION 3: Copper being reduced by heating in hydrogen
Copper(II) *oxide + hydrogen* ⇨ *copper + water*
$CuO(s) + H_2(g) ⇨ Cu(s) + H_2O(g)$

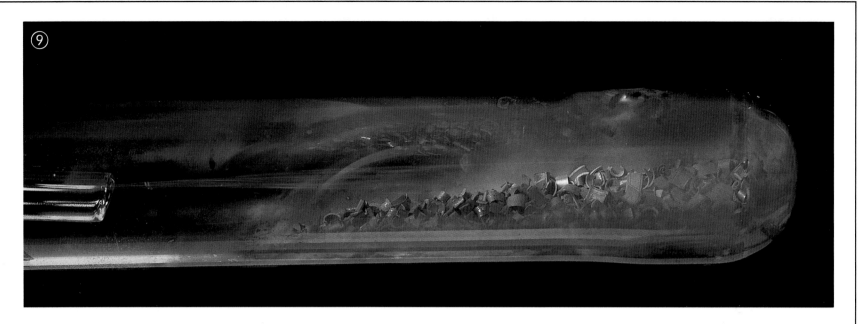

⑨

Remarks

Oxygen is never gained or lost during these reactions. When the hydrogen reduces the copper oxide, it combines with the oxygen it has removed and forms water (steam). Thus a reducing agent is oxidized during the process of reduction (⑩).

The copper oxide is an oxidizing agent and is reduced to copper.

⑩

$$Copper(II)\ oxide + hydrogen \rightsquigarrow copper + water$$
$$CuO(s) \quad + \quad H_2(g) \quad \rightsquigarrow \quad Cu(s) + H_2O(g)$$

Reduction

Oxidation

The hydrogen is a reducing agent and is oxidized to water.

Each reduction is accompanied by an oxidation, and each oxidation is accompanied by a reduction. The two processes always go together. This is why, to emphasize this fact, oxidation and reduction processes are usually referred to as "redox" (using the first letters of reduction and oxidation). In any equation one reactant (the reducing agent) gains oxygen, while the other reactant (the oxidizing agent) loses oxygen.

Substances that are reducing agents do not have to be devoid of oxygen themselves. For example, instead of hydrogen, carbon monoxide could be reacted with copper oxide, and the oxygen would still have been removed from the copper oxide.

EQUATION 4: Reduction of copper(II) oxide with carbon monoxide gas
$$Copper(II)\ oxide + carbon\ monoxide \rightsquigarrow copper\ metal + carbon\ dioxide$$
$$CuO(s) + CO(g) \rightsquigarrow Cu(s) + CO_2(g)$$

Carbon as a reducing agent

Carbon is a nonmetal in Group 4 of the Periodic Table. There are several forms of carbon. Some, like charcoal and coke, are important reducing agents in the presence of metals and are widely used in metal refining (see page 20). In the presence of a plentiful supply of oxygen the carbon is itself oxidized (it burns) to form carbon dioxide.

Demonstration: reducing steam with carbon

The reducing effect of carbon is apparent only when it is very hot. Thus this demonstration requires the use of a laboratory furnace designed to allow carbon to be heated nearly to white-hot.

Carbon, in the form of charcoal lumps, is placed in a heat-resistant silica tube inside the furnace (①). A supply of steam is provided by heating a metal container partly filled with water, using

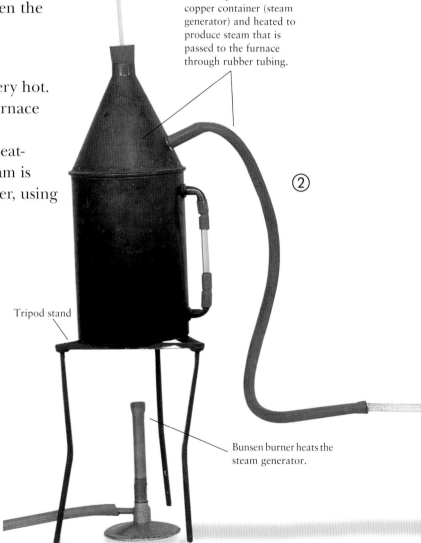

Safety tube

Water is placed in a copper container (steam generator) and heated to produce steam that is passed to the furnace through rubber tubing.

②

Tripod stand

Bunsen burner heats the steam generator.

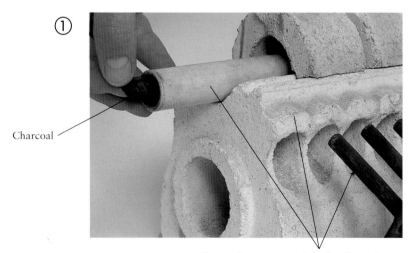

①

Charcoal

Carbon furnace consisting of a silica tube containing pieces of charcoal. This is heated by gas jets. Heat is conserved by surrounding the apparatus in a ceramic liner.

a Bunsen flame. The steam generator and the silica tube in the furnace are connected with flexible tubing (②).

In the furnace the carbon reduces the steam to hydrogen and is itself oxidized to carbon monoxide (③). The gases are collected in a gas jar over water (④).

The reaction of steam and water is an example of an ENDOTHERMIC REACTION, i.e., a reaction that takes in heat, so heat energy has to be continually applied using the furnace.

The mixture is known as water gas and is a one-to-one (by volume) mixture of hydrogen and carbon monoxide. If <u>air</u> is passed over very hot carbon as a reducing agent, the result is a mixture mainly of carbon monoxide and nitrogen known as producer gas. In this case the reaction is EXOTHERMIC (gives off heat).

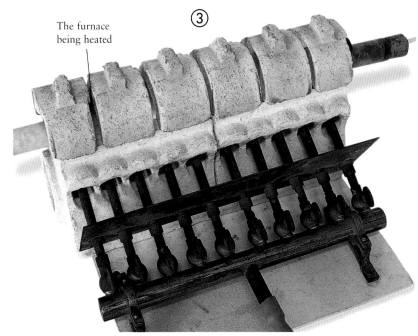

The furnace being heated ③

The steam is passed over the charcoal in the furnace.

EQUATION: Reduction of steam using carbon
Water + carbon ⇨ *carbon monoxide + hydrogen*
$H_2O(g) \rightarrow CO(g) + H_2(g)$

④

Water gas is collected over water in a gas jar seated on a beehive shelf in a water-filled PNEUMATIC TROUGH.

Reducing metal oxides

The oxides of the more reactive metals require strong reducing agents and high temperatures to reduce them. The standard industrial practice is to use a furnace.

Demonstration 1: reduction of iron(III) oxide using aluminum

Iron(III) oxide cannot be reduced (refined) to iron at room temperature or even with the heat of a Bunsen flame. For the reduction process to work, temperatures of about 2000°C are required, and these can only be obtained in a special furnace or by setting up a chemical reaction that releases sufficient heat (is sufficiently exothermic) to reduce the iron as used here.

In this demonstration iron(III) oxide is mixed with powdered aluminum and placed in an old boiling tube (since it will be destroyed). Aluminum is used as a reducing agent, but no reaction takes place at room temperature.

Some barium peroxide powder is placed in a hollow formed in the surface of this mixture, and a fuse of magnesium ribbon is pushed into the barium peroxide (①). The boiling tube is pushed into sand in an old tin can.

The magnesium fuse is then ignited, and the magnesium begins to burn with a brilliant white light. The fuse quickly burns down into the barium peroxide, and the heat causes the barium peroxide to decompose

and release oxygen. At this stage the demonstration resembles a Roman candle firework (②).

Enough heat energy is produced by this reaction to raise the temperature of the aluminum powder sufficiently that it will react with, and compete for the oxygen in, the iron(III) oxide (③). The aluminum reduces the iron(III) oxide to molten (liquid) elemental iron. This is a highly exothermic reaction. This additional heat raises the temperature of the molten metal to in excess of 2000°C. The high temperature also

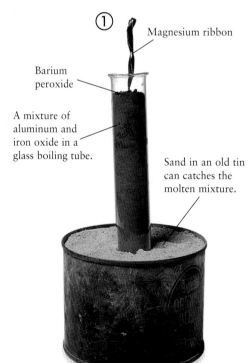

① Magnesium ribbon

Barium peroxide

A mixture of aluminum and iron oxide in a glass boiling tube.

Sand in an old tin can catches the molten mixture.

②

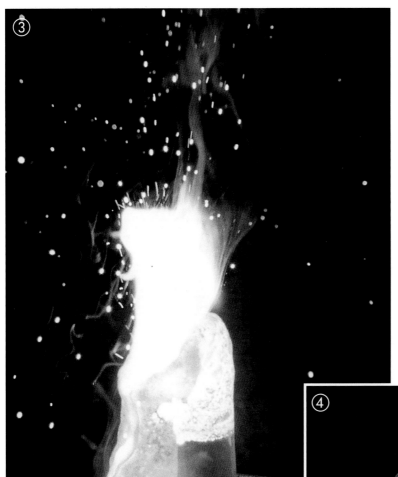

melts the boiling tube, and the molten mixture is safely collected in the sand (④).

While the iron(III) oxide is reduced, the aluminum in turn is oxidized to aluminum oxide. The aluminum oxide is a lightweight, fine powder that is easily carried upward by the rising currents of hot air as a white smoke.

Once cool, the glass can be knocked away to reveal the iron (⑤).

Remarks

Extremely high temperatures are reached during this demonstration, and so it could not safely be done in a laboratory. Instead, it was conducted in the open air, away from any flammable materials, and under close supervision. The supervisor and photographer were wearing appropriate safety equipment, and there were no spectators nearby.

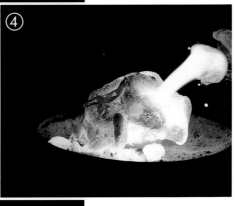

Refined iron with glass coating

EQUATION: Reduction of iron(III) oxide to iron

Iron(III) *oxide + aluminum* ⇨ *iron + aluminum oxide*

$$Fe_2O_3(s) + 2Al(s) \Rightarrow 2Fe(s) + Al_2O_3(s)$$

Demonstration 2: reduction of copper(II) oxide using carbon

A quantity of black copper oxide (copper(II) oxide, CuO) is placed on a ceramic dish. A similar quantity of charcoal is ground into a powder using a pestle and mortar, transferred to the dish, and mixed thoroughly with the copper oxide (⑥). The mixing is important because as much of the oxide as possible needs to be in contact with the carbon reducing agent.

The mixture of copper oxide and carbon is heated very strongly using a Bunsen flame (⑦). The carbon reduces some of the oxide and forms orange-colored copper that can be seen in patches where the substances make contact (⑧). Colorless carbon monoxide gas is given off during this reaction.

Remarks

Because the temperatures required are not as high as for iron, it is just possible to refine copper using carbon in a Bunsen flame. When left to cool, the copper is oxidized rapidly back to copper oxide by the oxygen in the surrounding air (⑨).

To prevent oxidation, a reducing environment has to be maintained until the copper has cooled. The use of a reduction tube, through which is passed a reducing gas such as carbon monoxide or hydrogen, is a more effective procedure (see page 12).

⑥ Carbon in the form of charcoal
Copper(II) oxide
Crucible
Pipe-clay triangle
Tripod stand

⑦ Bunsen flame

EQUATION: Reduction of copper(II) oxide to copper

Copper(II) *oxide + carbon* ⇨ *copper + carbon monoxide*

$CuO(s) + C(s)$ ⇨ $Cu(s) + CO(g)$

Redox in iron-making: the blast furnace

A blast furnace is a tall oven in which the conditions are controlled so that the iron ORE (iron(III) oxide) entering the top is progressively reduced (oxygen is removed) to iron metal that flows to the bottom.

Modern blast furnaces are designed to run continuously. They are charged with a mixture of iron ore, coke, and limestone at the top of the furnace. Each ton of iron uses up about three-quarters of a ton of coke and a quarter of a ton of limestone.

The smelting process

The ore must be reduced, and the resulting molten iron must be separated from any waste rock. This is achieved through the process called SMELTING.

First, oxygen is blown into the bottom of the furnace. The coke, which is almost entirely carbon, is oxidized by the oxygen and produces carbon dioxide gas, a reaction that also gives out heat.

As the carbon dioxide bubbles up through the furnace, it reacts with more of the coke in the mixture and is reduced to carbon monoxide gas. It is this hot carbon monoxide in the middle of the furnace that reacts with the iron ore (also in the middle of the furnace), reducing it to yield liquid iron.

Iron and waste materials (SLAG) have different densities and are drawn off separately at the bottom of the furnace.

EQUATION: Oxidation of coke

Carbon + oxygen ⇨ carbon dioxide

$C(s) + O_2(g) ⇨ CO_2(g)$

EQUATION: Carbon dioxide is reduced

Carbon dioxide + carbon ⇨ carbon monoxide

$CO_2(g) + C(s) ⇨ 2CO(s)$

EQUATION: Iron(III) oxide is reduced

Iron oxide(III) + carbon monoxide ⇨ iron metal + carbon dioxide

$Fe_2O_3(s) + 3CO(g) ⇨ 2Fe(l) + 3CO_2(g)$

Elements produced by industry using reduction and oxidation

REDUCTION

Element	Ore	Industrial process
Cu	Copper(II) sulfide (CuS)	Smelter $CuS(s) + O_2(g) ⇨ Cu(s) + SO_2(g)$
Fe	Iron(III) oxide (Fe_2O_3)	Blast furnace $Fe_2O_3(s) + 3CO(g) ⇨ 2Fe(l) + 3CO_2(g)$
Na	Sodium chloride (NaCl)	Electrolytic cell, Downs process $2NaCl(s) ⇨ 2Na(l) + Cl_2(g)$
Al	Bauxite (Al_2O_3)	Electrolytic cell, Hall process $2Al_2O_3(l) + 3C(s) ⇨ 4Al(l) + 3CO_2(g)$

OXIDATION

Element	Ore	Industrial process
S	Hydrogen sulfide (H_2S)	Claus process $2H_2S(g) + 3SO_2(g) + 2H_2O(g)$ then $2H_2S(g) + SO_2(g) ⇨ 3S(g) + 2H_2O(g)$
Cl	Brine (NaCl)	Diaphragm cell $2NaCl(aq) ⇨ 2Na(l) + Cl_2(g)$

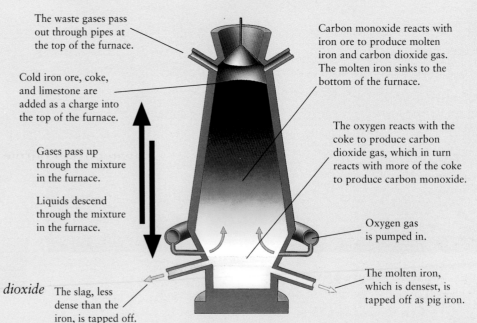

The waste gases pass out through pipes at the top of the furnace.

Cold iron ore, coke, and limestone are added as a charge into the top of the furnace.

Gases pass up through the mixture in the furnace.

Liquids descend through the mixture in the furnace.

Carbon monoxide reacts with iron ore to produce molten iron and carbon dioxide gas. The molten iron sinks to the bottom of the furnace.

The oxygen reacts with the coke to produce carbon dioxide gas, which in turn reacts with more of the coke to produce carbon monoxide.

Oxygen gas is pumped in.

The molten iron, which is densest, is tapped off as pig iron.

The slag, less dense than the iron, is tapped off.

Oxidizing agents

There is a wide range of oxidizing agents or oxidizers. Two of the three main mineral acids — concentrated sulfuric acid and concentrated nitric acid — are both oxidizing agents that are used to react with the less reactive metals. In the laboratory other important oxidizing agents are potassium permanganate, potassium dichromate, hydrogen peroxide, and the halogens (see page 28).

Demonstration 1: potassium permanganate as a colored oxidizing agent

Potassium permanganate is a very useful oxidizing agent for demonstrating redox reactions because it is a common reagent with a high OXIDATION STATE (potassium permanganate is manganate(VII), that is, it is associated with a change of 7 electrons). As it is reduced, the manganate changes through a number of different states of oxidation, or oxidation states (see also page 36), as manganate(VII) (purple), manganate(VI) (green), manganate(IV) (black), and manganate(II) (colorless) These distinctive colors make it much easier to see the progress of any oxidation reaction. Of course, this does not prevent us from using the manganate in more quantitative demonstrations, as the titration on page 24 shows.

The starting point for use of the manganate ion as an oxidizing agent is often its highest oxidation state as manganate(VII) in purple potassium permanganate.

If purple potassium permanganate solution is made alkaline with sodium hydroxide solution and is poured into a test tube containing hexene (a colorless hydrocarbon compound) (①), the liquid in the test tube immediately turns green (②) because the manganate ion has oxidized the hexene and, at the same time, has itself been reduced from (purple) manganate(VII) to (green) manganate(VI) (③ shows a comparison).

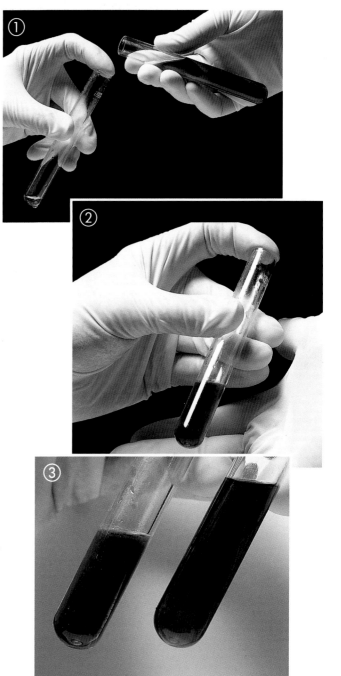

Demonstration 2: a redox titration

One way of finding out the strength of an oxidizing agent is to titrate it against a reducing agent. The standard method of TITRATION involves a BURETTE, in this case containing the oxidizing agent, and a conical flask (chosen because it is easy to swirl the contents in such flasks), which is used here to hold the reducing agent (④).

A known amount of reducing agent, which has been acidified by addition of dilute sulfuric acid, is put into the conical flask using a PIPETTE.

In this demonstration potassium permanganate (potassium manganate(VII)) acts as both the oxidizing agent and the indicator. While there is an excess of reducing agent in the conical flask, the drops of permanganate entering the flask will be reduced almost instantly from purple manganate(VII) to colorless manganese(II), $Mn^{2+}(aq)$.

The initial reading on the burette is recorded, and then, using the tap, drops of potassium permanganate are run from the burette into the conical flask (⑤). The conical flask is swirled after each addition in order to disperse the permanganate. As soon as the reducing agent has been completely used up, the next drops of permanganate entering the flask will remain unreduced and so will retain the purple permanganate color (⑥). This end point is therefore determined as soon as the solution remains pink. At this stage the reading of the burette is taken again, so that the total volume of permanganate used in the titration is known.

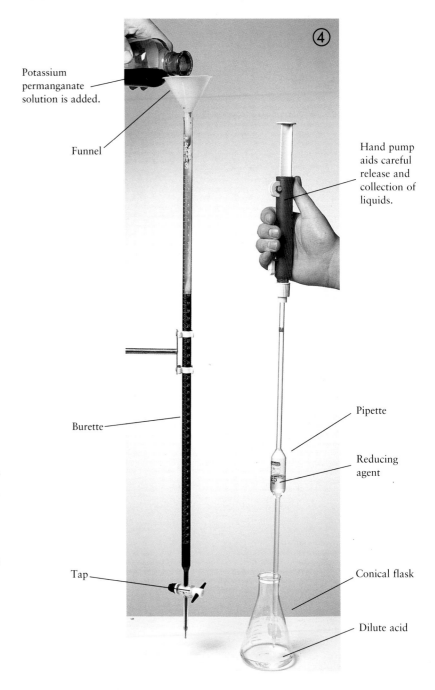

④

Potassium permanganate solution is added.

Funnel

Hand pump aids careful release and collection of liquids.

Burette

Pipette

Reducing agent

Tap

Conical flask

Dilute acid

⑤

The permanganate has been reduced from manganate(VII) to manganate(II) during this reaction, and in doing so each manganate ion has gained five electrons (VII to II).

Manganate ions are reduced to manganese ions

$$MnO_4^- + 8H^+ + 5e^- \Rightarrow Mn^{2+} + 4H_2O$$

Since we know the volume of the reducing agent, we can calculate its concentration if we know how many electrons it can lose, or conversely, if we know its concentration, we can discover how many electrons are involved in its oxidation.

So, for example, if the reducing agent is iron(II) sulfate then the iron(II) is oxidized to iron(III) and loses one electron:

Iron(II) ions are oxidized to iron(III) ions

$$Fe^{2+} \Rightarrow Fe^{3+} + e^-$$

Five iron(II) ions are therefore required to react with each manganate(VII) ion in the reaction.

The purple potassium permanganate that is added from the burette is reduced to colourless manganese(II) until the end point is reached.

⑥

The end point has been reached when the solution stays pink.

Demonstration 3: hydrogen peroxide as an oxidizing agent

Hydrogen peroxide, like potassium permanganate, is a compound containing a large proportion of oxygen. It is therefore an important oxidizing agent.

The first step of this demonstration is to produce an INDICATOR that is sensitive to changes in the balance between oxidation and reduction. To do this, 25 cm³ of (colorless) potassium iodide solution are first placed in each of three separate beakers. Then 10 drops of (colorless) starch are dropped into each beaker. The reaction of iodine and the starch creates a blue (complex) precipitate (①). The blue iodine will turn colorless when iodine is reduced to iodide ions, and the solution will turn blue again when iodide is

oxidized back to iodine. This property makes the starch and iodine solution an appropriate indicator.

To see the oxidizing effect of hydrogen peroxide, the solution must be in its reduced state. A known amount of reducing agent (in this case 2 cm³ of sodium thiosulfate solution) is first added and stirred into each of the beakers. Enough has been added that the iodine is reduced, and the solution turns clear (②). All three beakers are now ready to test the hydrogen peroxide.

As an oxidizing agent hydrogen peroxide counteracts the effect of the reducing agent. When it does so (it reaches the end point), the solution will turn blue again. Hydrogen peroxide works slowly, and so it takes some time for the effect to show. It can be timed with a stopwatch.

①

Starch

Colorless potassium iodide solution

Starch has been added.

②

Calibrated measuring cylinder

Sodium thiosulfate solution is added.

Sodium thiosulfate has been added.

In this demonstration three different solutions containing hydrogen peroxide were prepared in measuring cylinders (③). Each solution has the same total volume of 10 cm³. One measuring cylinder contains 10 cm³ of hydrogen peroxide, another contains 5 cm³ of hydrogen peroxide diluted with 5 cm³ of water, and a third contains 5 cm³ of hydrogen peroxide and of sulfuric acid. These solutions are added to separate beakers at the same time, and the stop watch is started (④).

The beaker to which the undiluted sulfuric acid is added turns deep blue instantly (⑤), showing that the acid has an important effect on the rate of oxidation of the solution. Of the other two beakers, the beaker with the higher concentration of hydrogen peroxide turns blue much faster (in about 4 minutes) (⑥) than the one that only had a diluted proportion (about 7 minutes) (⑦).

Remarks

The use of thiosulfate/peroxide in this way, with its instant change from colorless to blue, is a good method of showing not just that hydrogen peroxide is an effective oxidizing agent, and that it takes time for the reaction to proceed, but also that the rate at which the reaction takes place to completion varies with the amount of oxidizing agent. This is called the Harcourt-Essen or "clock" reaction because the reaction times are very accurately reproducible.

5 cm³ of hydrogen peroxide and 5 cm³ of sulfuric acid

Diluted solution of 5 cm³ of hydrogen peroxide and 5 cm³ of water

10 cm³ of hydrogen peroxide

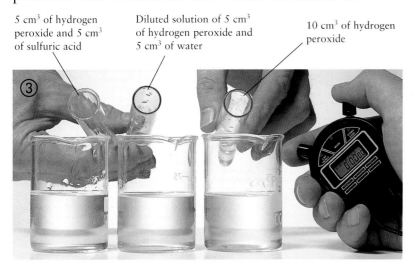

The halogens as oxidizing agents

The halogens are a family of very reactive nonmetallic chemical elements that belong to Group 7 of the Periodic Table. They include fluorine (F), chlorine (Cl), bromine (Br), and iodine (I).

The halogens can all behave as oxidizing agents, but their reactivity decreases down the group as the size of the atoms increases (from fluorine, to chlorine, to bromine, to iodine). The smaller atoms will even capture an electron (reduce) from the ions of larger members of the halogen family.

In the next five demonstrations you can see the relative strength of the halogens as oxidizing agents.

All the halogen gases are dangerous, and so all of these demonstrations are performed in a fume chamber. Fluorine is too reactive to be used in laboratory demonstrations.

Demonstration 1: chlorine as an oxidizing agent

A gas jar of chlorine (Cl_2) is prepared by reacting concentrated hydrochloric acid with potassium permanganate. The gas is collected in a gas jar by upward displacement of air.

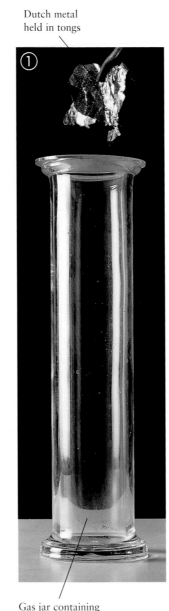

① Dutch metal held in tongs

Gas jar containing chlorine

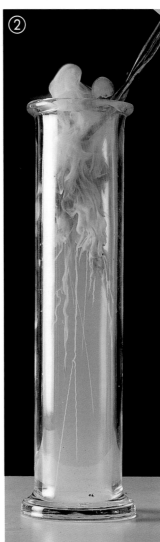

②

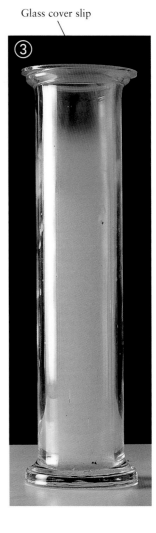

③ Glass cover slip

EQUATION: Chlorine reacts with finely divided copper
Chlorine + copper ➪ copper(II) chloride
$Cl_2(g) + Cu(s) ➪ CuCl_2(s)$

Finely divided copper (Dutch metal) is placed in the jaws of a pair of metal tongs, and the metal is introduced into the chlorine. The Dutch metal spontaneously COMBUSTS, showing that chlorine is an oxidizing agent (①)). The reaction produces fine particles of copper(II) chloride, seen as the dense smoke (②) that eventually fills the gas jar (③).

Demonstration 2: chlorine as an oxidizing agent

If concentrated sulfuric acid is added to sodium chloride in a test tube, a white froth is formed in the tube (④). Notice that the reaction does not produce any yellow-green chlorine. Instead, it produces a colorless gas, which is hydrochloric acid gas (HCl). Chlorine is such a strong oxidizing agent that the sulfuric acid (itself a strong oxidizing agent) cannot oxidize the chloride to chlorine.

The presence of hydrogen chloride gas can be tested for by holding a filter paper soaked in ammonia solution above the mouth of the tube (⑤). Steamy, white fumes of ammonium chloride indicate that the colorless gas in the tube is hydrogen chloride gas. This reaction is used in the standard laboratory preparation for hydrogen chloride.

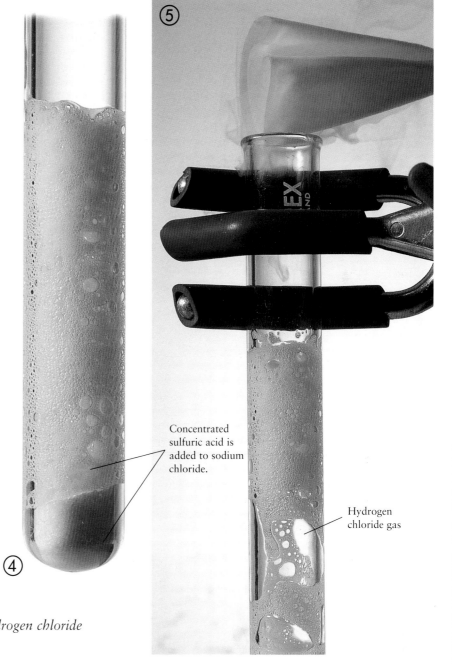

Concentrated sulfuric acid is added to sodium chloride.

Hydrogen chloride gas

EQUATION: Concentrated sulfuric acid with sodium chloride
Sulfuric acid + sodium chloride ⇨ sodium hydrogen sulfate + hydrogen chloride
$H_2SO_4(conc) + NaCl(s) ⇨ NaHSO_4(s) + HCl(g)$

Demonstration 3: bromine as an oxidizing agent

Bromine is not as strong an oxidizing agent as chlorine. When concentrated sulfuric acid is added to potassium bromide powder (⑥), hydrogen bromide (HBr) gas is produced. However, the sulfuric acid also oxidizes some of the hydrogen bromide to bromine gas (Br_2), resulting in a gas mixture (⑦).

Hydrogen bromide gas is colorless but can be tested for by placing a piece of filter paper soaked in ammonia near the top of the test tube. Like all compounds of hydrogen with halogens, the reaction of the acidic gas with the alkaline ammonia gas produces a white precipitate seen as a white smoke — in this case, ammonium bromide (⑧).

The brown gas is bromine. This can be differentiated from the other common brown gas, nitrogen dioxide, using moist pH paper. They are both acidic and so turn moist pH paper red. They both bleach the pH paper, but bromine does this more rapidly.

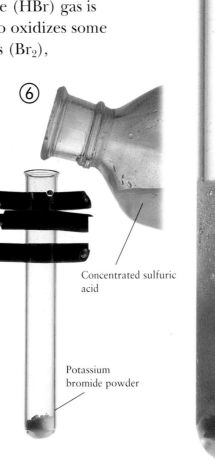

⑥

Concentrated sulfuric acid

Potassium bromide powder

⑦

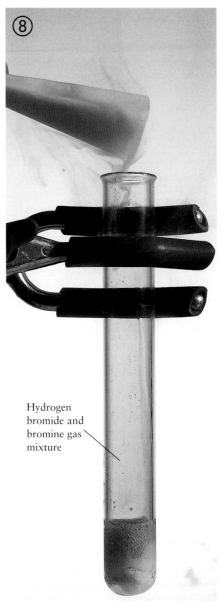

⑧

Hydrogen bromide and bromine gas mixture

EQUATION 1: Concentrated sulfuric acid with potassium bromide
Sulfuric acid + potassium bromide ⇨ potassium hydrogen sulfate + hydrogen bromide
$H_2SO_4(conc) + KBr(s) ⇨ KHSO_4(s) + HBr(g)$

EQUATION 2: Concentrated sulfuric acid with hydrogen bromide gas
Sulfuric acid + hydrogen bromide ⇨ water + sulfur dioxide + bromine
$H_2SO_4(conc) + HBr(g) ⇨ H_2O(l) + SO_2(sg) + Br_2(g)$

Demonstration 4: iodine as an oxidizing agent

Iodine is the least strong oxidizing agent of the halogens. When concentrated sulfuric acid is added to white potassium iodide powder in a test tube, no hydrogen iodide gas is produced, and only a dark brown effervescence occurs as the iodine vapor is liberated (⑨).

Placing a filter paper soaked in ammonia produces no steamy fumes as produced in the previous two demonstrations (⑩). Indeed, the sulfuric acid is a stronger oxidizing agent than the iodine and has completely oxidized the iodide to iodine. In this case iodide ion behaves as a reducing agent. As a result, hydrogen sulfide gas is produced, since the sulfuric acid is reduced to sulfur dioxide (SO_2) and then to hydrogen sulfide (H_2S).

The presence of sulfur dioxide or hydrogen sulfide can be tested by placing a piece of filter paper soaked in orange potassium dichromate near the open end of the tube. The color will change from orange to blue.

The reaction releases considerable amounts of heat (is strongly exothermic), and as a result the liquid in the tube bubbles violently. The purple iodine vapor SUBLIMES back to iodine crystals in the cooler area near the mouth of the tube.

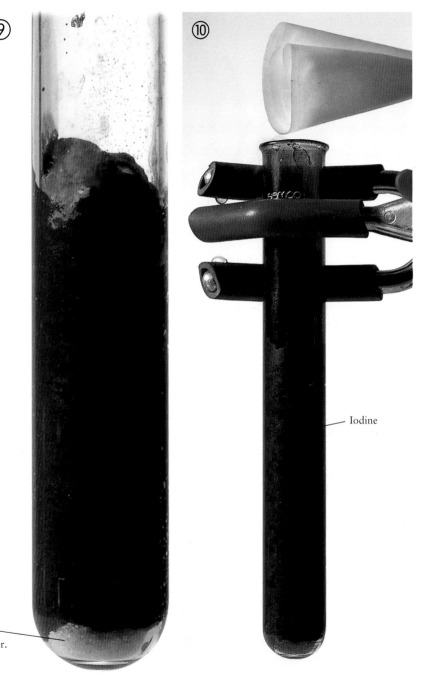

⑨

⑩

Iodine

Concentrated sulfuric acid is added to white potassium iodide powder.

Demonstration 5: reduction and oxidation of iodine

Oxidizing agent and reducing agent are relative terms given to substances. Many substances can actually act either as oxidizing agents or as reducing agents depending on the reactant they are placed with. For example, a substance that is a weak oxidizing agent will behave as though it were a strong oxidizing agent when put into a reaction with a strong reducing agent. A substance that is a weak oxidizing agent will behave as though it were a reducing agent when placed in a reaction with a strong oxidizing agent.

Iodine is at the boundary between substances that would normally be classed as oxidizing agents and those that could be classified as reducing agents. So an iodide ion (I^-) can be used as a test for oxidizing agents (since it becomes oxidized to iodine) because virtually all other oxidizing agents are stronger oxidizing agents than iodide. Similarly, you can use iodine (I_2) as a test for reducing agents because most reducing agents will reduce iodine to iodide.

As an example of this, if hydrogen sulfide gas (a strong reducing agent) is bubbled into iodine solution (⑪), the iodine is changed to colorless iodide, and the hydrogen sulfide will be oxidized to a PRECIPITATE of sulfur.

⑭

As the reaction proceeds, sulfur is precipitated as tiny yellow particles throughout the solution, making the contents of the test tube look milky (⑫). The yellow color of the sulfur becomes visible as the iodine is converted to colorless iodide, and the red-brown color of the solution is removed (⑬ & ⑭).

In contrast, if chlorine gas is bubbled through a colorless solution of potassium iodide (⑮), the iodide is oxidized to iodine as black particles (⑯) that make the solution look red-brown. The chlorine has oxidized the iodide to iodine. In turn, the chlorine has been reduced to chloride ions in solution.

EQUATION: Reduction of iodine to colorless iodide by hydrogen sulfide
Iodine ⇨ iodide
$I_2(aq) ⇨ 2I^-(aq)$

EQUATION: Oxidation of iodide to solid iodine by chlorine
Chlorine + iodide ⇨ chloride + iodine
$Cl_2(g) + 2I^-(aq) ⇨ 2Cl^-(aq) + I_2(s)$

⑮   ⑯

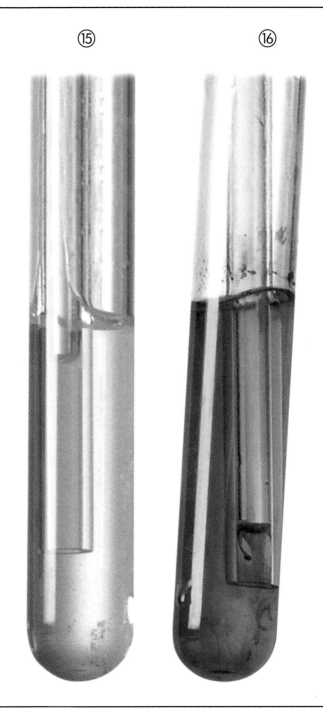

Reduction and oxidation in bleaching

BLEACHING AGENTS work either by oxidizing or reducing a substance from its colored to a colorless form.

A colored natural material gets its color from the way in which certain combinations of carbon atoms are BONDED together. Most synthetic dyes are also based on carbon compounds.

The coloring chemicals are able to absorb some wavelengths of light rays while reflecting others. When a bleach reacts with a colored material, the bleach breaks up or reduces some of the bonds, forming new substances that are not able to absorb light in the visible spectrum and so are colorless.

Demonstration 1: bleaches that are oxidizing agents, chlorine

Chlorine-based bleaches are oxidizing agents. Domestic bleach was traditionally made by passing chlorine gas over dry calcium oxide, producing calcium chlorate ($Ca(OCl)_2$). When added to water, this substance formed domestic bleach.

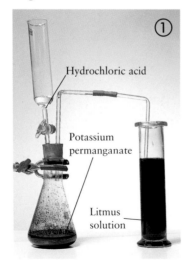

Hydrochloric acid

Potassium permanganate

Litmus solution

①

Powdered calcium chlorate, which can be added to water, and liquid solutions of sodium chlorate ($NaOCl$) are both sold as domestic bleach.

②

③

In this demonstration chlorine gas is produced by reacting hydrochloric acid with potassium permanganate in a flask. Chlorine is taken from the flask through a delivery tube and bubbled through a gas jar containing LITMUS solution as a dye (①). As the chlorine is passed through the solution, the litmus is bleached, and the liquid gradually clears (②, ③, & ④).

Demonstration 2: bleaches that are reducing agents, sulfur dioxide

Reducing bleaches include sulfur dioxide and sodium sulfite. Sulfur dioxide is used as an industrial bleach, especially for wood pulp.

In this demonstration sodium sulfite is placed in the end of a test tube. Dilute hydrochloric acid is added from a pipette (⑤). The reaction produces sulfur dioxide gas.

The sulfur dioxide is passed over a fresh, purple pansy flower (⑥). Within two minutes the flower is bleached, turning yellow (⑦) and then completely white (colorless).

④

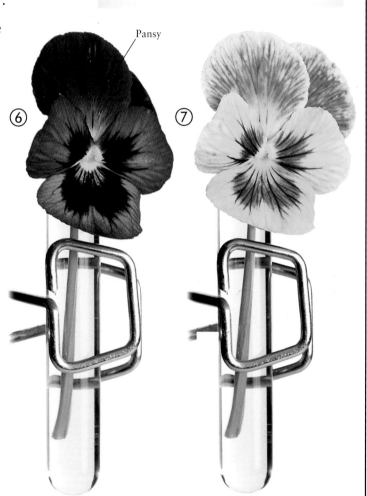

Pansy

⑥ ⑦

Colors that show oxidation and reduction

Some substances are oxidized in a number of stages known as oxidation states. The oxidation state is shown by an oxidation number, which is written in roman numerals. For example, manganate(VII) shows the manganate to have an oxidation number of 7.

Manganate(VII) is commonly known as permanganate. The "per" in permanganate means that the manganate is in its highest oxidation state. The high oxidation state (and plentiful supply of oxygen) makes it a powerful oxidizing agent.

Oxidation numbers increase during oxidation and decrease during reduction. So, as the manganate(VII) is reduced, it gains electrons, and its oxidation number decreases. The lowest oxidation number for manganese apart from the element itself (0) is most commonly 2, written as manganese(II).

Demonstration 1: oxidation states of potassium manganate

Manganate changes color as it changes oxidation state, as can be seen with the laboratory preparation of potassium permanganate. Potassium permanganate is commonly used in the laboratory and is stored as a purple, crystalline solid. Because of the way it changes color, and because it is a powerful oxidizing agent, potassium permanganate is used in several demonstrations in this book (see page 23).

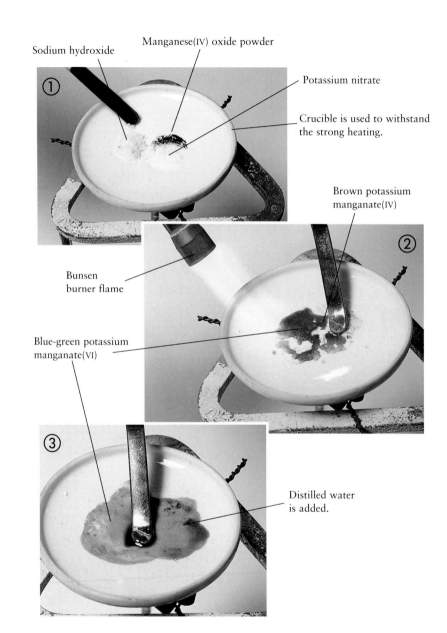

Sodium hydroxide

Manganese(IV) oxide powder

① Potassium nitrate

Crucible is used to withstand the strong heating.

Brown potassium manganate(IV)

②

Bunsen burner flame

Blue-green potassium manganate(VI)

③

Distilled water is added.

Notice that in the reactions below, the potassium ions in potassium manganate are SPECTATOR IONS and play no part in the reaction.

In this demonstration some brown manganese(IV) oxide is added to white potassium nitrate and white sodium hydroxide (①). The potassium nitrate will act as an oxidizing agent, changing the manganese(IV) to manganese(VI) and finally to manganese(VII). Sodium hydroxide is added to make the mixture alkaline and easily molten.

As the three powders are mixed and heated, a reaction takes place that produces a bluish-green paste (②). Oxidation has already taken place to some extent since some green manganese(VI) is already being produced. The complete reaction can be achieved by heating the paste (③).

The blue-green compound is allowed to cool, then transferred to a beaker by dissolving in water. Now the solution is clearly blue-green (④).

At this point the solution is acidified by adding dilute sulfuric acid. This makes the solution turn reddish-purple, which is manganate(VII) (⑤). However, brown manganese(IV) oxide is also produced and becomes visible when left to stand for a few minutes (⑥).

Remarks

The starting powder manganese(IV) and the final brown suspension look different because of the small particle size (COLLOID).

⑤

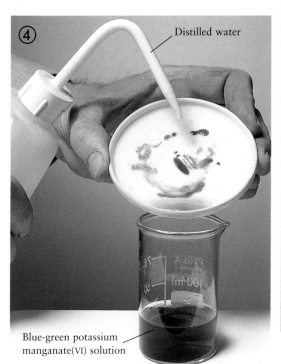

④

Distilled water

Blue-green potassium manganate(VI) solution

Dilute sulfuric acid

Deep purple potassium manganate(VII)

⑥

Mixture of purple potassium manganate(VII) with manganese(IV) oxide brown in suspension

Demonstration 2: oxidation states of vanadium

Concentrated hydrochloric acid is added to ammonium vanadate in a test tube (①). A piece of tin is then added (②), which makes it effervesce with small streams of bubbles of hydrogen.

The tin and concentrated acid make up a reducing system that reduces the vanadate from its highest oxidation state (vanadium(V)), to vanadium(IV), then to vanadium(III), and finally to vanadium(II).

Each of these stable oxidation states has a different color. There are also additional colors produced as the

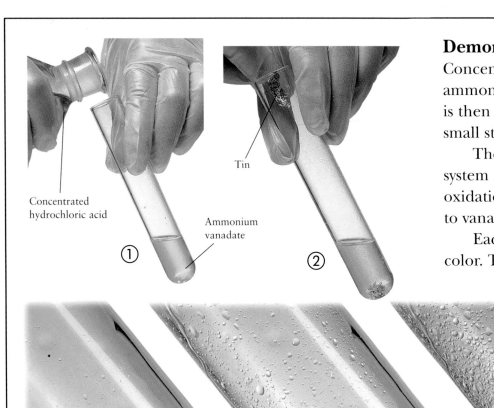

Concentrated hydrochloric acid

Ammonium vanadate

Tin

①

②

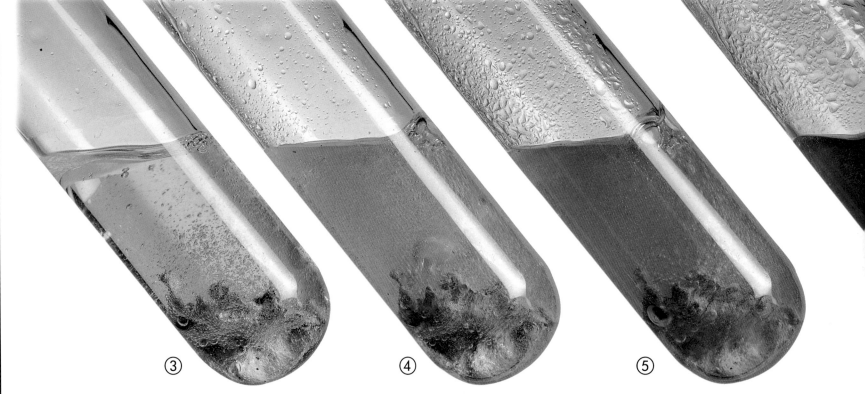

③

④

⑤

vanadium is reduced from one stable oxidation state to another. These transitional colors are made up of a mixture of colors that, in part, comes from the color remaining from one stable oxidation state and, in part, from the color from the new oxidation state. For example, vanadium appears green as it changes from yellow vanadium(V) to blue vanadium(IV). The genuine green oxidation state of vanadium, however, is vanadium(III).

These oxidation states and their transitional colors are shown across the bottom of these two pages:

③ Vanadium(V), oxidation state 5, yellow.
④ Transitional, green (a mixture of yellow and blue).
⑤ Vanadium(IV), oxidation state 4, blue.
⑥ Transitional, blue-green (a mixture of blue and green).
⑦ Vanadium(III), oxidation state 3, green.
⑧ Transitional, light violet (a mixture of green and violet).
⑨ Vanadium(II), oxidation state 2, violet.

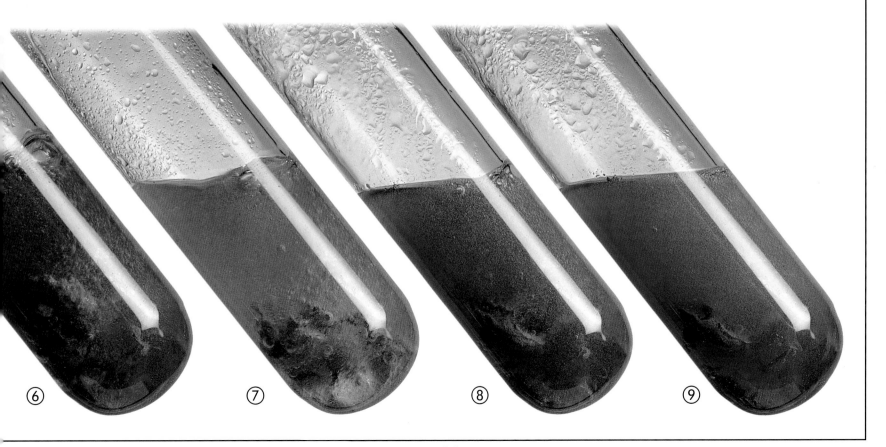

⑥　　　⑦　　　⑧　　　⑨

METALS

Metals can act as reducing agents. They can lose electrons in a redox reaction to form positively charged ions (CATIONS).

For example, when a piece of zinc metal is placed in dilute hydrochloric acid, a vigorous reaction takes place even at room temperature (①). Bubbles of gas are released, and some of the zinc "dissolves."

This is a redox reaction in which the zinc atoms (Zn) give up electrons to form zinc ions (Zn^{2+}). The zinc ions pass into the solution. At the same time, the released electrons are taken up by some of the hydrogen ions (H^+) in the acid solution near the metal. These hydrogen ions are reduced to atoms, which pair up to form molecules of hydrogen gas (H_2).

Zinc + hydrochloric acid ⇨ zinc chloride + hydrogen
$Zn(s) + 2HCl(aq) ⇨ ZnCl_2(aq) + H_2(g)$

In this redox reaction the zinc metal is the reducing agent and displaces the hydrogen from the acid solution as hydrogen gas. This is also known as a DISPLACEMENT REACTION. (Note that in this case the hydrogen ion is an oxidizing agent, in contrast to the demonstration on page 12 where the molecule is a reducing agent.)

If the same demonstration is repeated using copper metal instead of the zinc, no reaction occurs. Unlike zinc, copper is a weaker reducing agent than hydrogen, and so no displacement take place. This reinforces our understanding that reduction and oxidation are dependent on the relative strengths of the reducing and oxidizing agents involved.

The relative strengths of metals as reducing agents can be predicted using the metal activity series below. Those metals above hydrogen in the series will reduce hydrogen ions from an acid solution, converting them to hydrogen gas. Those metals below hydrogen will not cause the hydrogen to be displaced.

THE METAL ACTIVITY SERIES

Element	Metallic form (reduced form)	Ionic form (oxidized form)	Reactivity	Reducing or oxidizing power
Potassium	K	K^+		*Most strongly reducing or least strongly oxidizing*
Sodium	Na	Na^+		
Calcium	Ca	Ca^{2+}		
Magnesium	Mg	Mg^{2+}		
Aluminum	Al	Al^{3+}		
Manganese	Mn	Mn^{2+}		
Chromium	Cr	Cr^{2+}		
Zinc	Zn	Zn^{2+}		
Iron	Fe	Fe^{2+}	*Increasing reactivity*	
Cadmium	Cd	Cd^{2+}		
Tin	Sn	Sn^{2+}		
Lead	Pb	Pb^{2+}		
Hydrogen	H_2	H^+		
Copper	Cu	Cu^{2+}		
Mercury	Hg	Hg^{2+}		*Least strongly reducing or most strongly oxidizing*
Silver	Ag	Ag^+		
Gold	Au	Au^+		
Platinum	Pt	Pt^+		

(Above) The relative position of the metal to hydrogen in the activity series tells us whether the metal can produce hydrogen gas when reacted with an acid. Those above hydrogen in the series will reduce hydrogen ions in the acid to liberate hydrogen gas. Those below hydrogen in the table will not.

Strip of
zinc metal

Bubbles of
hydrogen gas

①

Dilute
hydrochloric acid

②

During displacement
copper ions are reduced
to copper atoms that
form a layer on the zinc.

Copper sulfate
solution contains
copper(II) ions.

Strip of zinc
metal is made
of zinc atoms.

Displacement reactions between metals

The activity series can be used to predict which metal will reduce and therefore displace the ions of another metal from a (salt) solution.

If a strip of zinc is placed in a solution containing copper ions (such as copper(II) sulfate), then a reaction occurs (②). As can be seen from the activity table, the zinc is a more powerful reducing agent than the copper. Indeed, some zinc atoms (Zn) on the surface of the strip are oxidized and give up electrons to form zinc ions (Zn^{2+}), which disperse into the solution. The copper ions (Cu^{2+}) near the zinc surface take up these free electrons and, in turn, form neutral copper atoms (Cu). These copper atoms can be seen initially as a black and finally orange deposit on the zinc strip submerged in the solution. This redox reaction can be represented by the following equation:

Zinc atoms + copper ions ⇨ zinc ions + copper atoms
$Zn(s) + Cu^{2+}(aq) ⇨ Zn^{2+}(aq) + Cu(s)$

The copper ion is the oxidizing agent, and the metallic zinc is the reducing agent. The zinc is oxidized from an oxidation state of 0 to +2. At the same time, the copper ion is reduced from an oxidation state of +2 to 0. In the process a zinc atom loses 2 electrons, and a copper ion gains those 2 electrons.

For any pair of metals involved in such a reaction, the one higher up the activity series will reduce or <u>displace</u> the other. There are many further demonstrations of this on pages 43 to 59 that can be used to make a displacement matrix that confirms the activity series of metals.

Because displacement reactions occur spontaneously and involve the transfer of electrons, they are the basis for the reactions in some chemical cells or batteries.

ELECTROCHEMISTRY

ELECTROCHEMISTRY is concerned both with reactions that produce an electric current and with the use of electricity to cause a chemical reaction. Both involve reduction and oxidation reactions.

The container in which these reactions take place is called a cell or ELECTROCHEMICAL CELL.

The cell is filled with a liquid that conducts electricity, called an ELECTROLYTE. The objects that conduct electricity into or out of the cell are called ELECTRODES. These are normally made from a material such as graphite (carbon) or platinum that does not react with the electrolyte.

Chemical cells that produce electricity

The reaction between zinc and copper on page 41 is a very simple chemical cell that produces electricity. The electrons that are exchanged as part of redox reactions can be passed through an external wire in an orderly fashion to make a current (see pages 60 to 63).

Electrolytic cells

Cells that use electricity to cause a chemical reaction in an electrolyte are called ELECTROLYTIC CELLS. The electrolyte is electrolyzed, or split up, in a process called ELECTROLYSIS (see page 64).

The electric current causes ions in the liquid to move to the electrodes. There the ions are reduced or oxidized.

John Frederic Daniell

John Frederic Daniell (1790–1845) was a British scientist most famous for inventing the first reliable source of direct current electricity.

In 1831 Daniell was appointed the first professor of chemistry at King's College, London, England. Here, he worked on electrochemistry, inventing the Daniell cell in 1836. He called it a constant battery because it maintained a steady voltage.

Previously, batteries had been made using zinc and copper electrodes, but although these gave high voltages, they could not maintain a steady current for very long. Daniell discovered that this effect was due to the production of hydrogen bubbles on the copper electrode. The bubbles gradually insulated the electrode from the electrolyte.

Daniell's new cell used two half-cells connected together by a salt bridge (see page 62). No gases are evolved in this cell, and so the current continues to flow steadily.

(Above) Copper is purified using electrolysis. Here copper cathodes, heavily plated with copper, are lifted from the electrolytic cells.

Creating a displacement matrix

The ability for a metal to displace another can be demonstrated by placing a strip or rod of one metal in a solution containing ions of the other metal. This has already been shown on page 41. Displacement can be observed.

The 17 demonstrations shown on the next 16 pages have been conducted systematically using six metals to construct the displacement matrix below. This illustrates the relative strengths of each metal as a reducing agent. The matrix confirms the activity series shown on page 40. The individual reactions that formed the basis of the matrix are shown with each demonstration on the following pages.

To make each demonstration comparable, the same bottle was used with similar volumes of metal and salt solution.

Small glass bottle allows easy observation.

Metal to be tested as a reducing agent

Solution containing ions of metal whose displacement is being determined.

The salt solutions used in the demonstrations on the following pages contain not only positively charged metal ions (cations) but also negatively charged ions (anions). These anions, such as sulfate and nitrate ions, are spectator ions; that is, they play no part in the reaction. This is why they are not shown in the ionic equations. This makes it easier to focus on the essential process — the NET IONIC REACTION.

(Right) This displacement matrix shows metals in order of decreasing strength as reducing agents (i.e., decreasing reactivity).

A check shows where metal atoms from the solid will reduce, and so displace, the ions of a less reactive metal from a solution (i.e., an appropriate salt solution).

✔ = Displacement takes place. The metal atoms shown down the left of the table will displace the metal ion shown across the top of the table.

✖ = Reaction does not take place.

50 = Page on which reaction is demonstrated.

DISPLACEMENT REACTION MATRIX						
Metal ions **Metal atoms**	Mg^{2+}	Zn^{2+}	Fe^{2+}	Pb^{2+}	Cu^{2+}	Ag^{+}
Magnesium (Mg)	✖	✔ 45	✔ 46	✔ 47	✔ 48	✔ 49
Zinc (Zn)	✖ 44	✖	✔ 50	✔ 51	✔ 52	✔ 53
Iron (Fe)	✖	✖	✖	✔ 54	✔ 54	✔ 56
Lead (Pb)	✖	✖	✖	✖	✔ 57	✔ 58
Copper (Cu)	✖	✖ 44	✖	✖	✖	✔ 58
Silver (Ag)	✖	✖	✖	✖	✖	✖

Decreasing strength as a reducing agent (decreasing reactivity)

Demonstration 1: zinc and magnesium

A piece of zinc is placed in colorless magnesium sulfate solution (①).

Result: No reaction occurs.

Conclusion: Zinc cannot displace magnesium from the solution, and so magnesium is a stronger reducing agent than zinc.

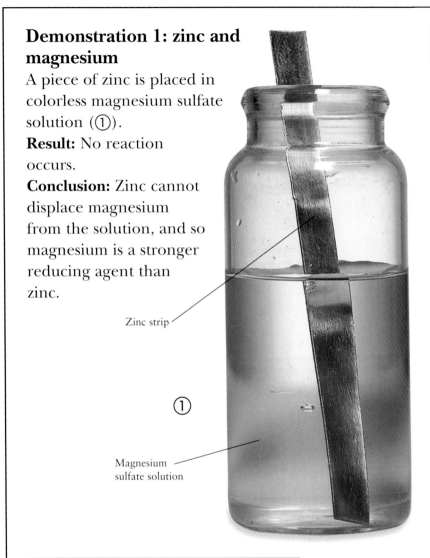

Zinc strip

①

Magnesium sulfate solution

Demonstration 2: copper and zinc

A piece of copper is placed in colorless zinc sulfate solution (②).

Result: No reaction occurs.

Conclusion: Copper cannot displace zinc from the solution, and so zinc is a stronger reducing agent than copper.

Copper strip

②

Zinc sulfate solution

DISPLACEMENT REACTION MATRIX (SEE ALSO PAGE 43)						
Metal ions / Metals	Mg^{2+}	Zn^{2+}	Fe^{2+}	Pb^{2+}	Cu^{2+}	Ag^+
Magnesium (Mg)	✘	✔	✔	✔	✔	✔
Zinc (Zn)	✘	✘	✔	✔	✔	✔
Iron (Fe)	✘	✘	✘	✔	✔	✔
Lead (Pb)	✘	✘	✘	✘	✔	✔
Copper (Cu)	✘	✘	✘	✘	✘	✔
Silver (Ag)	✘	✘	✘	✘	✘	✘

DISPLACEMENT REACTION MATRIX (SEE ALSO PAGE 43)						
Metal ions / Metals	Mg^{2+}	Zn^{2+}	Fe^{2+}	Pb^{2+}	Cu^{2+}	Ag^+
Magnesium (Mg)	✘	✔	✔	✔	✔	✔
Zinc (Zn)	✘	✘	✔	✔	✔	✔
Iron (Fe)	✘	✘	✘	✔	✔	✔
Lead (Pb)	✘	✘	✘	✘	✔	✔
Copper (Cu)	✘	✘	✘	✘	✘	✔
Silver (Ag)	✘	✘	✘	✘	✘	✘

Demonstration 3: magnesium and zinc

A piece of magnesium ribbon is placed in colorless zinc sulfate solution (③).

Result: The appearance of the surface of the magnesium under the solution changes rapidly (④).

Conclusion: Magnesium displaces zinc, and so magnesium is a stronger reducing agent than zinc.

Explanation: Magnesium atoms are oxidized, and zinc ions are reduced.

$$Mg(s) + Zn^{2+}(aq) \leftrightarrow Mg^{2+}(aq) + Zn(s)$$

The magnesium metal displaces zinc from the zinc sulfate solution. Zinc is precipitated on the surface of the magnesium ribbon and appears black since the very small particles reflect very little light in any one direction.

As the metal particles grow in size, they may look more like the bulk material (this is seen most easily in the case of silver on page 49). Although this is not visible in the picture, the underlying magnesium metal has become colorless magnesium ions in solution (If the bottle is shaken, the precipitated zinc will easily fall off since it is not attached firmly to the remaining magnesium. This is most clearly seen in the demonstration on page 47.)

Because magnesium reacts very slowly with water at room temperature, and because this reaction is more rapid if the magnesium is in contact with a less reactive metal, where magnesium is in contact with precipitated zinc, bubbles of hydrogen may be observed.

Magnesium ribbon

③

Zinc sulfate solution

④

DISPLACEMENT REACTION MATRIX (SEE ALSO PAGE 43)						
Metal ions / Metals	Mg^{2+}	Zn^{2+}	Fe^{2+}	Pb^{2+}	Cu^{2+}	Ag^+
Magnesium (Mg)	✘	✔	✔	✔	✔	✔
Zinc (Zn)	✘	✘	✔	✔	✔	✔
Iron (Fe)	✘	✘	✘	✔	✔	✔
Lead (Pb)	✘	✘	✘	✘	✔	✔
Copper (Cu)	✘	✘	✘	✘	✘	✔
Silver (Ag)	✘	✘	✘	✘	✘	✘

Demonstration 4: magnesium and iron

A piece of magnesium ribbon is placed in an almost colorless iron(II) sulfate solution (⑤).

Result: The appearance of the surface of the magnesium under the solution changes rapidly (⑥).

Conclusion: Magnesium is a stronger reducing agent than iron.

Explanation: Magnesium atoms are oxidized, and iron(II) ions are reduced.

$$Mg(s) + Fe^{2+}(aq) \leftrightarrow Mg^{2+}(aq) + Fe(s)$$

The magnesium metal displaces iron from the iron(II) sulfate solution. Iron is precipitated on the surface of the magnesium ribbon, and hydrogen gas is evolved. The reaction in this demonstration was more vigorous than that shown in the previous demonstration. The greater the difference in reducing power between the two metals, the more rapid the reaction is expected to be.

The turbulence resulting from the evolution of hydrogen dislodges the small particles of iron precipitated around the magnesium ribbon, and they fall away (⑦).

⑥

⑦

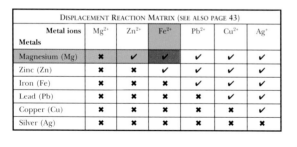

⑤

Magnesium ribbon

Iron(II) sulfate solution

Displacement Reaction Matrix (see also page 43)						
Metal ions / Metals	Mg²⁺	Zn²⁺	Fe²⁺	Pb²⁺	Cu²⁺	Ag⁺
Magnesium (Mg)	✘	✔	✔	✔	✔	✔
Zinc (Zn)	✘	✘	✔	✔	✔	✔
Iron (Fe)	✘	✘	✘	✔	✔	✔
Lead (Pb)	✘	✘	✘	✘	✔	✔
Copper (Cu)	✘	✘	✘	✘	✘	✔
Silver (Ag)	✘	✘	✘	✘	✘	✘

Demonstration 5: magnesium and lead

A piece of magnesium ribbon is placed in colorless lead nitrate solution (⑧).

Result: The appearance of the surface of the magnesium under the solution changes very rapidly (⑨ & ⑩).

Conclusion: Magnesium is a stronger reducing agent than lead.

Explanation: Magnesium atoms are oxidized, and lead(II) ions are reduced.

$$Mg(s) + Pb^{2+}(aq) \rightarrow Mg^{2+}(aq) + Pb(s)$$

The magnesium metal displaces lead from the lead nitrate solution. Lead is precipitated very rapidly on the surface of the magnesium ribbon. The particle size increases until reflection from the surface of the lead crystals is apparent as a shiny sheen (⑪).

Magnesium ribbon

Lead nitrate solution

Displacement Reaction Matrix (see also page 43)						
Metal ions / **Metals**	Mg^{2+}	Zn^{2+}	Fe^{2+}	Pb^{2+}	Cu^{2+}	Ag^+
Magnesium (Mg)	✗	✔	✔	✔	✔	✔
Zinc (Zn)	✗	✗	✔	✔	✔	✔
Iron (Fe)	✗	✗	✗	✔	✔	✔
Lead (Pb)	✗	✗	✗	✗	✔	✔
Copper (Cu)	✗	✗	✗	✗	✗	✔
Silver (Ag)	✗	✗	✗	✗	✗	✗

Demonstration 6: magnesium and copper

A piece of magnesium ribbon is placed in blue copper(II) sulfate solution ((12)).

Result: The appearance of the surface of the magnesium within the solution changes very rapidly ((13)).

Conclusion: Magnesium is a stronger reducing agent than copper.

Explanation: Magnesium atoms are oxidized, and copper(II) ions are reduced:

$$Mg(s) + Cu^{2+}(aq) \Rightarrow Mg^{2+}(aq) + Cu(s)$$

The magnesium metal displaces copper from the copper(II) sulfate solution. Copper is precipitated very rapidly on the surface of the magnesium ribbon, and hydrogen gas is evolved.

As precipitation continues, the particle size will increase until reflection from the surface of the copper crystals gives the solution a typical red-pink color. Enough blue copper(II) ions are removed eventually for the solution to become much paler.

(12)

Magnesium ribbon

Copper(II) sulfate solution

(13)

DISPLACEMENT REACTION MATRIX (SEE ALSO PAGE 43)						
Metal ions / **Metals**	Mg²⁺	Zn²⁺	Fe²⁺	Pb²⁺	Cu²⁺	Ag⁺
Magnesium (Mg)	✘	✔	✔	✔	✔	✔
Zinc (Zn)	✘	✘	✔	✔	✔	✔
Iron (Fe)	✘	✘	✘	✔	✔	✔
Lead (Pb)	✘	✘	✘	✘	✔	✔
Copper (Cu)	✘	✘	✘	✘	✘	✔
Silver (Ag)	✘	✘	✘	✘	✘	✘

Demonstration 7: magnesium and silver

A piece of magnesium ribbon is placed in colorless silver nitrate solution (⑭).

Result: The appearance of the surface of the magnesium within the solution changes almost instantly (⑮).

Conclusion: Magnesium is a stronger reducing agent than silver.

Explanation: Magnesium atoms are oxidized, and silver ions are reduced.

$$Mg(s) + 2Ag^+(aq) \Rightarrow Mg^{2+}(aq) + 2Ag(s)$$

The magnesium metal displaces silver from the silver nitrate solution. Silver is precipitated very rapidly on the surface of the magnesium ribbon. The particle size increases until reflection from the surface of the silver crystals is apparent as a METALLIC LUSTER (⑯).

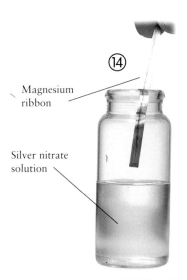

⑭

Magnesium ribbon

Silver nitrate solution

⑮

⑯

DISPLACEMENT REACTION MATRIX (SEE ALSO PAGE 43)						
Metal ions \ Metals	Mg^{2+}	Zn^{2+}	Fe^{2+}	Pb^{2+}	Cu^{2+}	Ag^+
Magnesium (Mg)	✗	✓	✓	✓	✓	✓
Zinc (Zn)	✗	✗	✓	✓	✓	✓
Iron (Fe)	✗	✗	✗	✓	✓	✓
Lead (Pb)	✗	✗	✗	✗	✓	✓
Copper (Cu)	✗	✗	✗	✗	✗	✓
Silver (Ag)	✗	✗	✗	✗	✗	✗

Demonstration 8: zinc and iron

A zinc strip is placed in almost colorless iron(II) sulfate solution.

Result: The appearance of the surface of the zinc within the solution changes rapidly (⑰).

Conclusion: Zinc is a stronger reducing agent than iron.

Explanation: Zinc atoms are oxidized, and iron(II) ions are reduced.

$$Zn(s) + Fe^{2+}(aq) \rightsquigarrow Zn^{2+}(aq) + Fe(s)$$

The zinc metal displaces iron from the iron(II) sulfate solution. Iron is precipitated on the surface of the zinc strip.

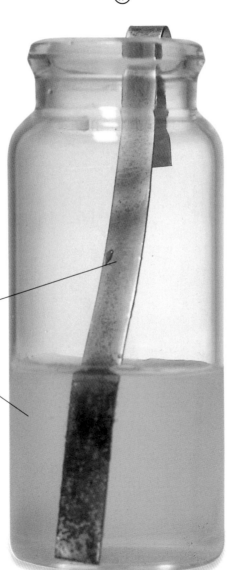

Zinc strip

Iron(II) sulfate solution

DISPLACEMENT REACTION MATRIX (SEE ALSO PAGE 43)						
Metal ions Metals	Mg²⁺	Zn²⁺	Fe²⁺	Pb²⁺	Cu²⁺	Ag⁺
Magnesium (Mg)	✘	✔	✔	✔	✔	✔
Zinc (Zn)	✘	✘	✔	✔	✔	✔
Iron (Fe)	✘	✘	✘	✔	✔	✔
Lead (Pb)	✘	✘	✘	✘	✔	✔
Copper (Cu)	✘	✘	✘	✘	✘	✔
Silver (Ag)	✘	✘	✘	✘	✘	✘

Demonstration 9: zinc and lead

Zinc strip is placed in colorless lead nitrate solution (⑱).

Result: The appearance of the surface of the zinc under the solution changes rapidly (⑲ & ⑳).

Conclusion: Zinc is a stronger reducing agent than lead.

Explanation: Zinc atoms are oxidized, and lead(II) ions are reduced.

$$Zn(s) + Pb^{2+}(aq) \rightsquigarrow Zn^{2+}(aq) + Pb(s)$$

The zinc metal displaces lead from the lead nitrate solution. Lead is precipitated on the surface of the zinc strip.

DISPLACEMENT REACTION MATRIX (SEE ALSO PAGE 43)						
Metal ions Metals	Mg²⁺	Zn²⁺	Fe²⁺	Pb²⁺	Cu²⁺	Ag⁺
Magnesium (Mg)	✘	✔	✔	✔	✔	✔
Zinc (Zn)	✘	✘	✔	✔	✔	✔
Iron (Fe)	✘	✘	✘	✔	✔	✔
Lead (Pb)	✘	✘	✘	✘	✔	✔
Copper (Cu)	✘	✘	✘	✘	✘	✔
Silver (Ag)	✘	✘	✘	✘	✘	✘

⑳

Zinc strip

⑱

⑲

Lead nitrate solution

51

Demonstration 10: zinc and copper

A piece of zinc strip is placed in blue copper(II) sulfate solution (㉑).

Result: The appearance of the surface of the zinc under the solution changes rapidly (㉒).

Conclusion: Zinc is a stronger reducing agent than copper.

Explanation: Zinc atoms are oxidized, and copper(II) ions are reduced.

$$Zn(s) + Cu^{2+}(aq) \Rightarrow Zn^{2+}(aq) + Cu(s)$$

The zinc metal displaces copper from the copper(II) sulfate solution. Copper is precipitated on the surface of the zinc strip.

The copper(II) sulfate solution eventually turns paler, and the precipitate becomes orange.

㉑

㉒

Zinc strip

Copper(II) sulfate solution

DISPLACEMENT REACTION MATRIX (SEE ALSO PAGE 43)						
Metal ions Metals	Mg^{2+}	Zn^{2+}	Fe^{2+}	Pb^{2+}	Cu^{2+}	Ag^+
Magnesium (Mg)	✘	✔	✔	✔	✔	✔
Zinc (Zn)	✘	✘	✔	✔	✔	✔
Iron (Fe)	✘	✘	✘	✔	✔	✔
Lead (Pb)	✘	✘	✘	✘	✔	✔
Copper (Cu)	✘	✘	✘	✘	✘	✔
Silver (Ag)	✘	✘	✘	✘	✘	✘

Demonstration 11: zinc and silver

A piece of zinc strip is placed in colorless silver nitrate solution (㉓).

Result: The appearance of the surface of the zinc within the solution changes almost instantly (㉔).

Conclusion: Zinc is a stronger reducing agent than silver.

Explanation: Zinc atoms are oxidized, and silver ions are reduced.

$$Zn(s) + 2Ag^+(aq) \Leftrightarrow Zn^{2+}(aq) + 2Ag(s)$$

The zinc metal displaces silver from the silver nitrate solution. Silver is precipitated on the surface of the zinc strip. The particle size increases until reflection from the surface of the silver crystals is apparent as a metallic luster (㉕).

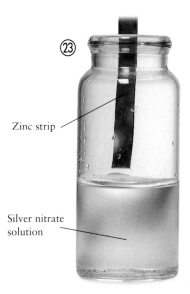

㉓

Zinc strip

Silver nitrate solution

㉔

㉕

DISPLACEMENT REACTION MATRIX (SEE ALSO PAGE 43)						
Metal ions / Metals	Mg²⁺	Zn²⁺	Fe²⁺	Pb²⁺	Cu²⁺	Ag⁺
Magnesium (Mg)	✘	✔	✔	✔	✔	✔
Zinc (Zn)	✘	✘	✔	✔	✔	✔
Iron (Fe)	✘	✘	✘	✔	✔	✔
Lead (Pb)	✘	✘	✘	✘	✔	✔
Copper (Cu)	✘	✘	✘	✘	✘	✔
Silver (Ag)	✘	✘	✘	✘	✘	✘

Demonstration 12: iron and lead

An iron nail is placed in colorless lead nitrate solution.

Result: The appearance of the surface of the iron nail under the solution changes slowly (㉖).

Conclusion: Iron is a stronger reducing agent than lead.

Explanation: Iron atoms are oxidized, and lead(II) ions are reduced.

$$Fe(s) + Pb^{2+}(aq) \rightarrow Fe^{2+}(aq) + Pb(s)$$

The iron metal displaces lead from the lead nitrate solution. Lead is precipitated on the surface of the iron nail, giving it a darker-colored coating. However, this is quite a slow reaction as the lead is not all that different from the iron in terms of reactivity.

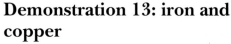

㉖

Iron nail

Lead nitrate solution

DISPLACEMENT REACTION MATRIX (SEE ALSO PAGE 43)						
Metal ions / Metals	Mg^{2+}	Zn^{2+}	Fe^{2+}	Pb^{2+}	Cu^{2+}	Ag^+
Magnesium (Mg)	✗	✔	✔	✔	✔	✔
Zinc (Zn)	✗	✗	✔	✔	✔	✔
Iron (Fe)	✗	✗	✗	✔	✔	✔
Lead (Pb)	✗	✗	✗	✗	✔	✔
Copper (Cu)	✗	✗	✗	✗	✗	✔
Silver (Ag)	✗	✗	✗	✗	✗	✗

Demonstration 13: iron and copper

An iron nail is placed in blue copper(II) sulfate solution (㉗).

Result: The appearance of the surface of the iron nail under the solution changes slowly (㉘).

Conclusion: Iron is a stronger reducing agent than copper.

Explanation: Iron atoms are oxidized, and copper(II) ions are reduced.

$$Fe(s) + Cu^{2+}(aq) \rightarrow Fe^{2+}(aq) + Cu(s)$$

The iron metal displaces copper from the copper(II) sulfate solution. Copper is precipitated on the surface of the iron nail.

Over several hours the blue color of the solution fades to a very pale green as the result of the formation of iron(II) ions. Oxidation of this solution by the oxygen of the air can cause the solution to appear yellow

DISPLACEMENT REACTION MATRIX (SEE ALSO PAGE 43)						
Metal ions / Metals	Mg^{2+}	Zn^{2+}	Fe^{2+}	Pb^{2+}	Cu^{2+}	Ag^+
Magnesium (Mg)	✗	✔	✔	✔	✔	✔
Zinc (Zn)	✗	✗	✔	✔	✔	✔
Iron (Fe)	✗	✗	✗	✔	✔	✔
Lead (Pb)	✗	✗	✗	✗	✔	✔
Copper (Cu)	✗	✗	✗	✗	✗	✔
Silver (Ag)	✗	✗	✗	✗	✗	✗

(in which case iron(III) ions have been formed).

The color of the precipitate changes from black to the characteristic red-pink of metallic copper as the particle size increases ().

Iron nail

Copper(II) sulfate solution

Demonstration 14: iron and silver

An iron nail is placed in dilute silver nitrate solution (③⓪).

Result: The appearance of the surface of the iron nail under the solution changes slowly (③①).

Conclusion: Iron is a stronger reducing agent than silver.

Explanation: Iron atoms are oxidized, and, silver ions are reduced.

$$Fe(s) + 2Ag^+(aq) \Leftrightarrow Fe^{2+}(aq) + 2Ag(s)$$

The iron metal displaces silver from the silver nitrate solution. Silver is precipitated in a shiny layer, plating the surface of the iron nail (③②). This effectively stops further reaction.

③⓪

Iron nail

Silver nitrate solution

③①

DISPLACEMENT REACTION MATRIX (SEE ALSO PAGE 43)						
Metal ions **Metals**	Mg^{2+}	Zn^{2+}	Fe^{2+}	Pb^{2+}	Cu^{2+}	Ag^+
Magnesium (Mg)	✘	✔	✔	✔	✔	✔
Zinc (Zn)	✘	✘	✔	✔	✔	✔
Iron (Fe)	✘	✘	✘	✔	✔	✔
Lead (Pb)	✘	✘	✘	✘	✔	✔
Copper (Cu)	✘	✘	✘	✘	✘	✔
Silver (Ag)	✘	✘	✘	✘	✘	✘

Demonstration 15: lead and copper

A piece of lead strip is placed in blue copper(II) sulfate solution.

Result: The appearance of the surface of the lead under the solution changes slowly (③③).

Conclusion: Lead is slightly stronger as a reducing agent compared with copper.

Explanation: Lead atoms are oxidized, and copper(II) ions are reduced.

$$Pb(s) + Cu^{2+}(aq) \leftrightarrows Pb^{2+}(aq) + Cu(s)$$

The lead metal displaces copper from the copper(II) sulfate solution. Red-pink colored copper is precipitated on the surface of the lead strip.

Lead strip

Copper(II) sulfate solution

DISPLACEMENT REACTION MATRIX (SEE ALSO PAGE 43)						
Metal ions **Metals**	Mg^{2+}	Zn^{2+}	Fe^{2+}	Pb^{2+}	Cu^{2+}	Ag^+
Magnesium (Mg)	✘	✔	✔	✔	✔	✔
Zinc (Zn)	✘	✘	✔	✔	✔	✔
Iron (Fe)	✘	✘	✘	✔	✔	✔
Lead (Pb)	✘	✘	✘	✘	✔	✔
Copper (Cu)	✘	✘	✘	✘	✘	✔
Silver (Ag)	✘	✘	✘	✘	✘	✘

Demonstration 16: lead and silver

A piece of lead strip is placed in colorless silver nitrate solution (㉞).

Result: The appearance of the surface of the lead within the solution changes slowly (㉟).

Conclusion: Lead is slightly stronger as a reducing agent compared with silver.

Explanation: Lead atoms are oxidized, and silver ions are reduced.

$$Pb(s) + 2Ag^+(aq) \Rightarrow Pb^{2+}(aq) + 2Ag(s)$$

The lead metal displaces silver from the silver nitrate solution. Silver is precipitated on the surface of the lead strip. The particle size increases until reflection from the surface of the silver crystals is apparent as a metallic luster (㊱).

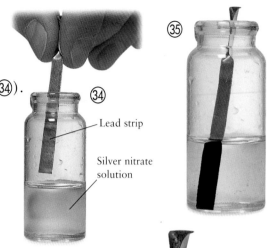

Lead strip

Silver nitrate solution

㉞

㉟

㊱

Demonstration 17: copper and silver

A copper strip is placed in colorless silver nitrate solution.

Result: The appearance of the surface of the copper within the solution changes slowly (㊲).

Conclusion: The copper is a slightly stronger reducing agent compared to silver.

Explanation: Copper atoms are oxidized, and silver ions are reduced.

$$Cu(s) + 2Ag^+(aq) \Rightarrow Cu^{2+}(aq) + 2Ag(s)$$

The copper metal displaces silver from the silver nitrate solution. Silver is precipitated on the surface of the copper strip. The particle size increases until reflection from the surface of the silver crystals is apparent as a metallic luster (㊳).

As the concentration of the copper ions in the solution increases, the solution appears distinctly blue (㊴).

DISPLACEMENT REACTION MATRIX (SEE ALSO PAGE 43)						
Metal ions / Metals	Mg^{2+}	Zn^{2+}	Fe^{2+}	Pb^{2+}	Cu^{2+}	Ag^+
Magnesium (Mg)	✘	✔	✔	✔	✔	✔
Zinc (Zn)	✘	✘	✔	✔	✔	✔
Iron (Fe)	✘	✘	✘	✔	✔	✔
Lead (Pb)	✘	✘	✘	✘	✔	✔
Copper (Cu)	✘	✘	✘	✘	✘	✔
Silver (Ag)	✘	✘	✘	✘	✘	✘

DISPLACEMENT REACTION MATRIX (SEE ALSO PAGE 43)						
Metal ions / Metals	Mg^{2+}	Zn^{2+}	Fe^{2+}	Pb^{2+}	Cu^{2+}	Ag^+
Magnesium (Mg)	✘	✔	✔	✔	✔	✔
Zinc (Zn)	✘	✘	✔	✔	✔	✔
Iron (Fe)	✘	✘	✘	✔	✔	✔
Lead (Pb)	✘	✘	✘	✘	✔	✔
Copper (Cu)	✘	✘	✘	✘	✘	✔
Silver (Ag)	✘	✘	✘	✘	✘	✘

37 Copper strip

38

39

Silver nitrate solution

59

A chemical cell and the movement of electrons

A simple electrochemical cell can be constructed to produce an electric current (see page 42). This is a type of battery. A redox reaction is used to produce a transfer of electrons that can be passed through an external wire in an orderly fashion to create an electric current. Unlike an electrolytic cell (see page 64), no external supply of electricity is used.

This demonstration of a chemical cell provides convincing evidence that oxidation and reduction are processes that involve the transfer of electrons and are not simply the addition or removal of oxygen and hydrogen.

Demonstration: an iodine-manganate cell

Two separate beakers filled with solutions (electrolytes) are connected by a SALT BRIDGE. An electrode is placed in each beaker, and the two electrodes are connected by a wire (①).

To make the salt bridge, a U-tube is filled with a concentrated solution of sodium sulfate; the ends are plugged with porous cotton and inverted so that each end is in a beaker. Neither the sodium ions nor the sulfate ions in the solution in the salt bridge play any part in the reaction, which is why they are chosen. They simply provide a conducting solution that is the chemical equivalent of a length of wire connecting the solutions in the two beakers.

The left-hand beaker contains purple potassium permanganate acidified with sulfuric acid, forming an oxidizing solution. The right-hand beaker contains a reducing solution of potassium iodide and starch (see also page 26), which is colorless. If electrons can be taken from the iodide ions, they will be oxidized to iodine. Since iodine reacts with starch to produce a blue color, it can be observed clearly and is an indicator of oxidation of the iodide.

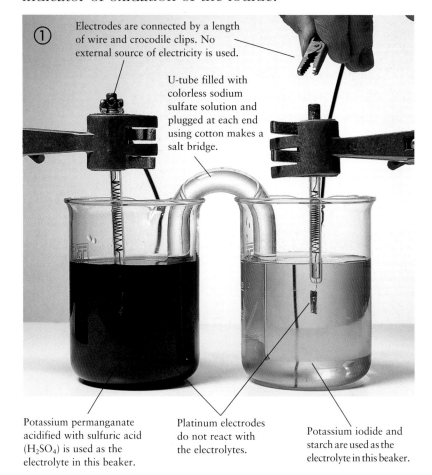

① Electrodes are connected by a length of wire and crocodile clips. No external source of electricity is used.

U-tube filled with colorless sodium sulfate solution and plugged at each end using cotton makes a salt bridge.

Potassium permanganate acidified with sulfuric acid (H_2SO_4) is used as the electrolyte in this beaker.

Platinum electrodes do not react with the electrolytes.

Potassium iodide and starch are used as the electrolyte in this beaker.

As soon as the length of wire is connected to each ELECTRODE, a change is seen (②). Trails of indicator begin to appear around the electrode in the right-hand beaker, showing that the iodide is being oxidized to iodine in this region. So, despite the two solutions being in separate beakers, electrons are being transferred between them, and the connecting wire has completed the circuit. The electrons pass out of the right-hand beaker from the oxidized iodide and through the external wire as a current to arrive at the left-hand beaker. In this solution permanganate gains electrons through the wire and is reduced to colorless manganese(II) ions. Ions pass the charge through the salt bridge.

EQUATION 1: At the electrode in the iodide beaker iodide ions are oxidized to form iodine molecules and release electrons to flow through the wire.

Iodine ions ⇨ iodine + electrons

$$2I^-(aq) \Rightarrow I_2(s) + 2e^-$$
electric current

EQUATION 2: At the electrode in the potassium permanganate beaker manganate(VII) ions are reduced by the electrons that arrive through the wire to form manganese(II) ions.

Potassium permanganate + hydrogen ions + electrons ⇨ manganese ions + water

$$2MnO_4^-(aq) + 8H^+(aq) + 5e^- \Rightarrow Mn^{2+}(aq) + 4H_2O(l)$$
electric current

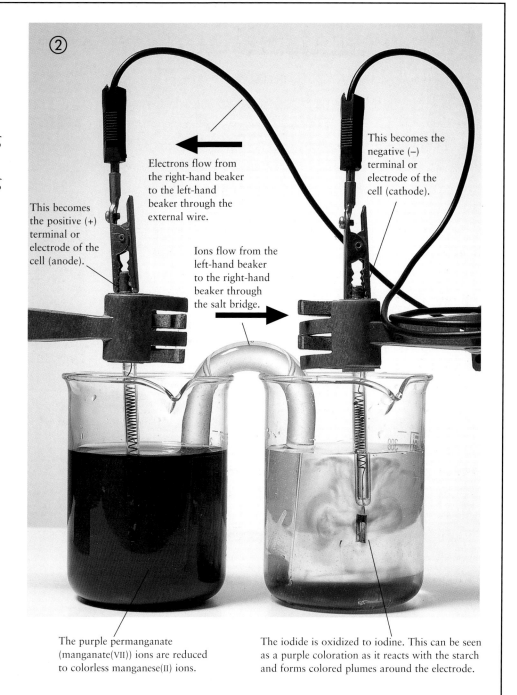

② Electrons flow from the right-hand beaker to the left-hand beaker through the external wire.

This becomes the positive (+) terminal or electrode of the cell (anode).

This becomes the negative (–) terminal or electrode of the cell (cathode).

Ions flow from the left-hand beaker to the right-hand beaker through the salt bridge.

The purple permanganate (manganate(VII)) ions are reduced to colorless manganese(II) ions.

The iodide is oxidized to iodine. This can be seen as a purple coloration as it reacts with the starch and forms colored plumes around the electrode.

The redox reactions in a Daniell cell (battery)

In the demonstration on page 60 we
have shown that connecting an oxidizing
system to a reducing system causes a flow
of ions through the salt bridge and
therefore a flow of electrons through the
wire. We have demonstrated the essential
features of a battery. Here is the
development of such a cell to show how,
by choosing the electrolytes and electrode
materials appropriately, we can produce a
battery that operates at a useful voltage.

Demonstration: a zinc-copper Daniell cell

In this demonstration the cell consists
of two beakers connected by a salt bridge
(①). The left-hand beaker contains an
electrolyte of zinc sulfate solution and a
zinc electrode. This electrode acts as
the ANODE of the cell (where oxidation
occurs — the negative terminal of the
battery).

In the right-hand beaker there is an
electrolyte of copper(II) sulfate solution
and an electrode of copper. This
electrode will act as the CATHODE of the
cell (where reduction occurs — the
positive terminal of the battery).

① Salt bridge

Zinc metal anode

Zinc sulfate solution

Copper cathode

Copper(II) sulfate solution

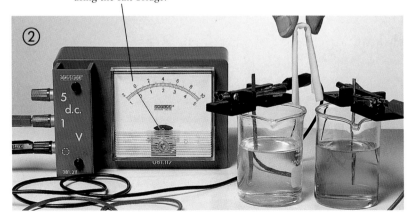

The volt meter reads 0 before
the two solutions are connected
using the salt bridge.

②

The salt bridge consists of a piece of folded filter paper that has been soaked in sodium sulfate solution. The ions of this solution play no part in the reaction; the role of the salt bridge is just to provide an unreacting electrical connection between the beakers.

The two electrodes are in series with a meter set up to read voltage (②). When connected, the meter reads 1.1 volts, characteristic of the voltage produced by the redox reaction of the two metals (③ & ④). The copper cathode becomes bright as it is plated with copper from the copper sulfate solution. At the same time, the copper sulfate solution becomes paler as the copper ions are used up. Eventually this will cause the flow of ions, and thus the current in the external circuit, to cease.

Remarks

The filter paper soaked in solution demonstrates that it is sufficient to have a dampened material as an electrolyte. From this it is an easy step to understand how "dry" batteries are able to work. The material used as a salt bridge in dry batteries is actually a fabric or paper impregnated with a suitable salt solution.

③

1.1 volts, the characteristic voltage of the zinc-copper Daniell cell

④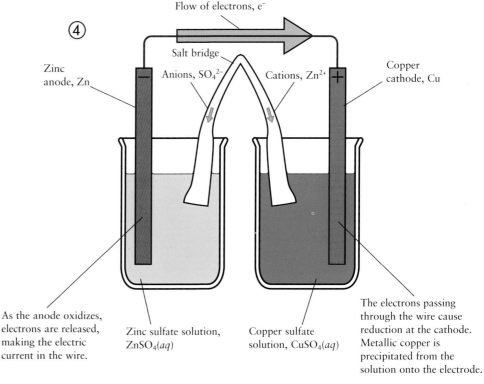

Flow of electrons, e⁻

Salt bridge

Zinc anode, Zn

Anions, SO_4^{2-}

Cations, Zn^{2+}

Copper cathode, Cu

As the anode oxidizes, electrons are released, making the electric current in the wire.

Zinc sulfate solution, $ZnSO_4(aq)$

Copper sulfate solution, $CuSO_4(aq)$

The electrons passing through the wire cause reduction at the cathode. Metallic copper is precipitated from the solution onto the electrode.

Oxidation

Zinc metal ⇨ zinc ions + electrons
$Zn(s) ⇨ Zn^{2+}(aq) + 2e^-$

Reduction

Copper ions + electrons ⇨ copper metal
$Cu^{2+}(aq) + 2e^- ⇨ Cu(s)$

Reduction and oxidation in an electrolytic cell

The processes of oxidation and reduction can be demonstrated when an external electric current is passed through an appropriate electrolyte in an electrolytic cell (see page 42).

Demonstration: electrolysis of sodium chloride

In this demonstration the cell is a clear, side-arm U-tube. The U-tube is filled with sodium chloride (NaCl) solution (brine, common salt dissolved in water), which is the electrolyte and colorless. A few drops of UNIVERSAL INDICATOR are added to the solution. The green coloration shows that the solution is neutral before electrolysis (①). The side arms of the U-tube allow the gases produced in the space above the solution to be led off for collection over water in boiling tubes.

Two carbon electrodes are held in the sodium chloride solution using stoppers that also seal and prevent gases escaping from the top of the U-tube. Carbon electrodes are used, since they will not react with the solution.

The electrodes are connected to a power pack. As soon as the electricity supply is applied, the Universal Indicator turns a deep violet around the left-hand electrode, showing reducing conditions. In contrast, the indicator around the right-hand electrode turns red, but is soon bleached to a pale yellow (②). The acid bleaching action suggests that the gas being given off is chlorine.

As the demonstration progresses, more and more of the electrolyte changes color. At the same time, more gas accumulates in the boiling tubes. In this demonstration hydrogen is liberated at the cathode (negative terminal), which in this case is on the left, and chlorine is liberated at the anode (positive terminal) on the right.

Even though exactly the same volume of gas is liberated vigorously at each electrode, there will be far less chlorine collected than hydrogen. This is because the chlorine is relatively soluble and will dissolve in the water initially.

Eventually all the solution is altered and is either bleached or violet (③).

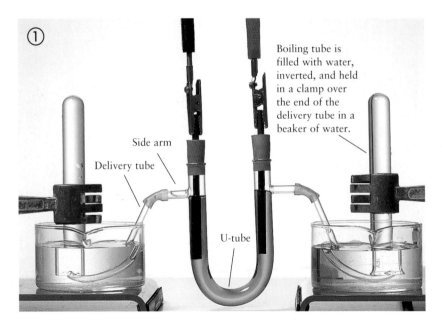

①

Boiling tube is filled with water, inverted, and held in a clamp over the end of the delivery tube in a beaker of water.

Side arm

Delivery tube

U-tube

The gas in the left-hand tube can be tested by removing the tube from the pneumatic trough and then bringing a lighted splint to the mouth of the tube. A loud pop indicates the presence of hydrogen.

The gas given off at the right-hand electrode is tested with a piece of filter paper soaked in potassium iodide solution. The solution on the filter paper is turned brown by the presence of chlorine (④ & ⑤).

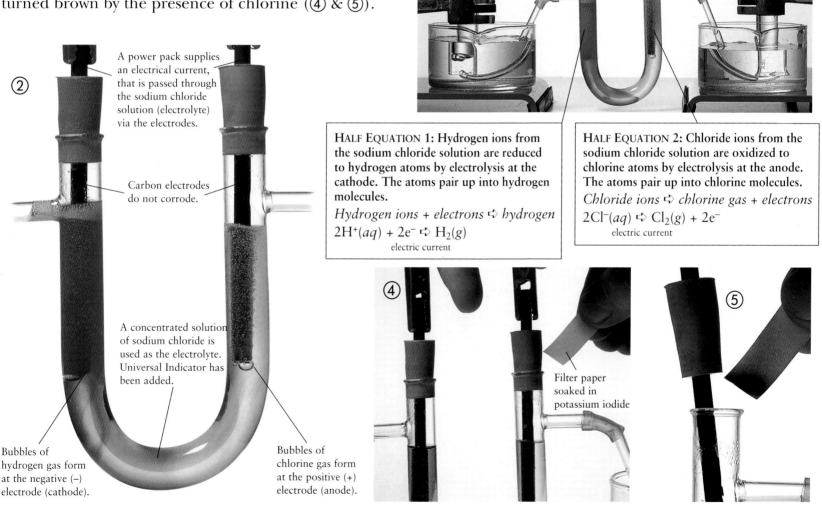

③

Colorless hydrogen gas is collected.

Yellow-green chlorine gas is collected.

②

A power pack supplies an electrical current, that is passed through the sodium chloride solution (electrolyte) via the electrodes.

Carbon electrodes do not corrode.

A concentrated solution of sodium chloride is used as the electrolyte. Universal Indicator has been added.

Bubbles of hydrogen gas form at the negative (−) electrode (cathode).

Bubbles of chlorine gas form at the positive (+) electrode (anode).

HALF EQUATION 1: Hydrogen ions from the sodium chloride solution are reduced to hydrogen atoms by electrolysis at the cathode. The atoms pair up into hydrogen molecules.

Hydrogen ions + electrons ⇨ hydrogen
$2H^+(aq) + 2e^- ⇨ H_2(g)$
electric current

HALF EQUATION 2: Chloride ions from the sodium chloride solution are oxidized to chlorine atoms by electrolysis at the anode. The atoms pair up into chlorine molecules.

Chloride ions ⇨ chlorine gas + electrons
$2Cl^-(aq) ⇨ Cl_2(g) + 2e^-$
electric current

④

⑤

Filter paper soaked in potassium iodide

MASTER GLOSSARY

absolute zero: the lowest possible temperature ($-273.15°C$).

absorption: the process by which a substance is soaked up. *See:* adsorption.

acid: a substance that can give a proton to another substance. Acids are compounds containing hydrogen that can attack and dissolve many substances. Acids are described as weak or strong, dilute or concentrated, mineral or organic. *Example:* hydrochloric acid (HCl). An acid in water can react with a base to form a salt and water.

acidic solution: a solution with a pH lower than 7. *See:* pH.

acidity: a general term for the strength of an acid in a solution.

acid radical: the negative ion left behind when an acid loses a hydrogen ion. *Example:* Cl^- in hydrochloric acid (HCl).

acid salt: An ACID SALT contains at least one hydrogen ion and can behave as an acid in chemical reactions. Acid salts are produced under conditions that do not allow complete neutralization of the acid. For example, sulfuric acid may react with a sodium compound to produce a normal sodium salt, sodium sulfate (Na_2SO_4), or it may retain some of the hydrogen, in which case it becomes the salt sodium hydrogen sulfate ($NaHSO_4$).

actinide series or actinide metals: a series of 15 similar radioactive elements between actinium and lawrencium. They are transition metals.

activated charcoal: a form of carbon made of tiny crystals of graphite that is made by heating organic matter in the absence of air. It is then further processed to increase its pore space and therefore its surface area. Its surface area is about 2000 m^2/g. Activated charcoal readily adsorbs many gases, and it is therefore widely used as a filter, for example, in gas masks.

activation energy: the energy required to make a reaction occur. The greater the activation energy of a reaction, the more its reaction rate depends on temperature. The activation energy of a reaction is useful because, if the rate of reaction is known at one temperature (for example, 100 °C) then the activation energy can be used to calculate the rate of reaction at another temperature (for example, at 400 °C) without actually doing the experiment.

adsorption: the process by which a surface adsorbs a substance. The substances involved are not chemically combined and can be separated. *See:* absorption.

alchemy: the traditional "art" of working with chemicals common in the Middle Ages. One of the main challenges for alchemists was to make gold from lead. Alchemy faded away as scientific chemistry was developed in the 17th century.

alcohol: an organic compound that contains a hydroxyl (OH) group. *Example:* ethanol (CH_3CH_2OH), also known as ethyl alcohol or grain alcohol.

alkali/alkaline: a base in (aqueous) solution. Alkalis react with or neutralize hydrogen ions in acids and have a pH greater than 7.0 because they contain relatively few hydrogen ions. *Example:* aqueous sodium hydroxide (NaOH). *See:* pH.

alkaline cell (or battery): a dry cell in which the electrolyte contains sodium or potassium hydroxide.

alkaline earth metal: a member of Group 2 of the Periodic Table. *Example:* calcium.

alkali metals: a member of Group 1 of the Periodic Table. *Example:* sodium.

alkane: a hydrocarbon with no carbon-to-carbon multiple bonds. *Example:* ethane, C_2H_6.

alkene: a hydrocarbon with at least one carbon-to-carbon double bond. *Example:* ethylene, C_2H_4.

alkyne: a hydrocarbon with at least one carbon-to-carbon triple bond. *Example:* acetylene, C_2H_2.

allotropes: alternative forms of an element that differ in the way the atoms are linked. *Example:* white and red phosphorus.

alloy: a mixture of a metal and various other elements. *Example:* brass is an alloy of copper and zinc.

amalgam: a liquid alloy of mercury with another metal.

amorphous: a solid in which the atoms are not arranged regularly (i.e., "glassy"). Compare crystalline.

amphoteric: a metal that will react with both acids and alkalis. *Example:* aluminum metal.

anhydrous: lacking water; water has been removed, for example by heating. (Opposite of anhydrous is hydrous or hydrated.) *Example:* copper(II) sulfate can be anhydrous ($CuSO_4$) or hydrated ($CuSO_4•5H_2O$).

anion: a negatively charged atom or group of atoms. *Examples:* chloride ion (Cl^-), hydroxide ion (OH^-). *Example:* aqueous sodium hydroxide (NaOH). *See:* pH.

anode: the electrode at which oxidation occurs; the negative terminal of a battery or the positive electrode of an electrolysis cell.

anodizing: a process that uses the effect of electrolysis to make a surface corrosion-resistant. *Example:* anodized aluminum.

antacid: a common name for any compound that reacts with stomach acid to neutralize it. *Example:* sodium hydrogen carbonate, also known as sodium bicarbonate.

antioxidant: a substance that reacts rapidly with radicals, thereby preventing oxidation of some other substance.

antibumping granules: small glass or ceramic beads designed to promote boiling without the development of large gas bubbles.

approximate relative atomic mass: *See:* relative atomic mass.

aqueous: a solution in which the solvent is water. Usually used as "aqueous solution." *Example:* aqueous solution of sodium hydroxide (NaOH(aq)).

aromatic hydrocarbons: compounds of carbon that have the benzene ring as part of their structure. *Examples:* benzene (C_6H_6), naphthalene ($C_{10}H_8$). They are known as aromatic because of their strong pungent smell.

atmospheric pressure: the pressure exerted by the gases in the air. Units of measurement are kilopascals (kPa), atmospheres (atm), millimeters of mercury (mm Hg), and Torr. Standard atmospheric pressure is 100 kPa, 1atm, 760 mm Hg or 760 Torr.

atom: the smallest particle of an element; a nucleus and its surrounding electrons.

atomic mass: the mass of an atom measured in atomic mass units (u). An atomic mass unit equals one twelfth of the atom of carbon-12. "Atomic mass" is now more generally used than "atomic weight." *Example:* the atomic mass of chlorine is about 35 u. *See:* atomic weight, relative atomic mass.

atomic number: also known as proton number. The number of electrons or the number of protons in an atom. *Example:* the atomic number of gold is 79.

atomic structure: the nucleus and the arrangement of electrons around it.

atomic weight: a common term used to mean the average molar mass of an element (g/mol). This is the mass per mole of atoms. *Example:* the atomic weight of chlorine is about 35 g/mol. *See:* atomic mass, mole.

base: a substance that can accept a proton from another substance. *Example:* aqueous ammonia ($NH_3(aq)$). A base can react with an acid in water to form a salt and water.

basic salt: a salt that contains at least one hydroxide ion. The hydroxide ion can then behave as a base in chemical reactions. *Example:* the reaction of hydrochloric acid (HCl) with the base aluminum hydroxide ($Al(OH)_3$) can form two basic salts, $Al(OH)_2Cl$ and $Al(OH)Cl_2$.

battery: a number of electrochemical cells placed in series.

bauxite: a hydrated impure oxide of aluminum ($Al_2O_3•xH_2O$, with the amount of water x being variable). It is the main ore used to obtain aluminum metal. The reddish brown color of bauxite is mainly caused by the iron oxide impurities it contains.

beehive shelf: an inverted earthenware bowl with a hole in the upper surface and a slot in the rim. Traditionally the earthenware was brown and looked similar to a beehive, hence its name. A delivery tube passes through the slot, and a gas jar is placed over the hole. This provides a convenient way to collect gas over water in a pneumatic trough.

bell jar: a tall glass jar with an open bottom and a wide, stoppered neck that is used in conjunction with a beehive shelf and a pneumatic trough in some experiments involving gases. The name derives from historic versions of the apparatus, which resembled a bell in shape.

blast furnace: a tall furnace charged with a mixture of iron ore, coke, and limestone and used for the refining of iron metal. The name comes from the strong blast of air introduced during smelting.

bleach: a substance that removes color from stains on materials either by oxidizing or reducing the staining compound. *Example:* sulfur dioxide (SO_2).

block: one of the main divisions of the Periodic Table. Blocks are named for the outermost occupied electron shell of an element. *Example:* the Transition Metals all belong to the d-block.

boiling point: the temperature at which a liquid boils, changing from a liquid to a gas. Boiling points change with atmospheric pressure. *Example:* The boiling point of pure water at standard atmospheric pressure is 100 °C.

boiling tube: A thin glass tube closed at one end and used for chemical tests. The composition and thickness of the glass is such that it cannot sustain very high temperatures and is intended for heating liquids to boiling point. *See:* side-arm boiling tube, test tube.

bond: chemical bonding is either a transfer or sharing of electrons by two or more atoms. There are a number of types of chemical bond, some very strong (such as covalent and ionic bonds), others weak (such as hydrogen bonds). Chemical bonds form because the linked molecule is more stable than the unlinked atoms from which it formed. *Example:* the hydrogen molecule (H_2) is more stable than single atoms of hydrogen, which is why hydrogen gas is always found as molecules of two hydrogen atoms.

Boyle's Law: At constant temperature, and for a given mass of gas, the volume of the gas (V) is inversely proportional to pressure that builds up (P): $P \propto 1/V$.

brine: a solution of salt (sodium chloride, NaCl) in water.

Büchner flask: a thick-walled side-arm flask designed to withstand the changes in pressure that occur when the flask is connected to a suction pump.

Büchner funnel: a special design of plastic or ceramic funnel that has a flat stage on which a filter paper can be placed. It is intended for use under suction with a Büchner funnel.

buffer (solution): a mixture of substances in solution that resists a change in the acidity or alkalinity of the solution when small amounts of an acid or alkali are added.

burette: a long, graduated glass tube with a tap at one end. A burette is used vertically, with the tap lowermost, as a reservoir for a chemical during titration.

burn: a combustion reaction in which a flame is produced. A flame occurs where *gases* combust and release heat and light. At least two gases are therefore required if there is to be a flame. *Example:* methane gas (CH_4) burns in oxygen gas (O_2) to produce carbon dioxide (CO_2) and water (H_2O) and give out heat and light.

calorimeter: an insulated container designed to prevent heat gain or loss with the environment and thus allow changes of temperature within reacting chemicals to be measured accurately. It is named after the old unit of heat, the calorie.

capillary: a very small diameter (glass) tube. Capillary tubing has a small enough diameter to allow surface tension effects to retain water within the tube.

capillary action: the tendency for a liquid to be sucked into small spaces, such as between objects and through narrow-pore tubes. The force to do this comes from surface tension.

carbohydrate: a compound containing only carbon, hydrogen and oxygen. Carbohydrates have the formula $C_n(H_2O)_n$, where n is variable. *Example:* glucose ($C_6H_{12}O_6$).

carbonate: a salt of carbonic acid. Carbonate ions have the chemical formula CO_3^{2-}. *Examples:* calcium nitrate $CaCO_3$ and sodium carbonate Na_2CO_3.

catalyst: a substance that speeds up a chemical reaction but itself remains unaltered at the end of the reaction. *Example:* copper in the reaction of hydrochloric acid with zinc.

catalytic converter: a device incorporated into some exhaust systems. The catalytic converter contains a framework or granules with a very large surface area and coated with catalysts that convert the pollutant gases passing over them into harmless products.

cathode: the electrode at which reduction occurs; the positive terminal of a battery or the negative electrode of an electrolysis cell.

cathodic protection: the technique of protecting a metal object by connecting it to a more readily oxidizable metal. The metal object being protected is made into the cathode of a cell. *Example:* iron can be protected by coupling it with magnesium. Iron forms the cathode and magnesium the anode.

cation: a positively charged ion. *Examples:* calcium ion (Ca^{2+}), ammonium ion (NH_4^+).

caustic: a substance that can cause burns if it touches the skin. *Example:* Sodium hydroxide, caustic soda (NaOH).

Celsius scale (°C): a temperature scale on which the freezing point of water is at 0 degrees, and the normal boiling point at standard atmospheric pressure is 100 degrees.

cell: a vessel containing two electrodes and an electrolyte that can act as an electrical conductor.

centrifuge: an instrument for spinning small samples very rapidly. The fast spin makes the components of a mixture that have a different density separate, as in filtration.

ceramic: a material based on clay minerals that has been heated so that it has chemically hardened.

chalcogens: the members of Group 6 of the Periodic Table: oxygen, sulfur, selenium and tellurium. The word comes from the Greek meaning "brass giver," because all these elements are found in copper ores, and copper is the most important metal in making brass.

change of state: a change between two of the three states of matter, solid, liquid, and gas. *Example:* when water evaporates it changes from a liquid to a gaseous state.

Charles's Law: The volume (V) of a given mass of gas at constant pressure is directly proportional to its absolute temperature (T): $V \propto T$.

chromatography: A separation technique uses the ability of surfaces to adsorb substances with different strengths. The substances with the least adherence to the surface move faster and leave behind those that adhere more strongly.

coagulation: a term describing the tendency of small particles to stick together in clumps.

coherent: meaning that a substance holds together or sticks together well, and without holes or other defects. *Example:* Aluminum appears unreactive because, as soon as new metal is exposed to air, it forms a very complete oxide coating, which then stops further reaction occurring.

coinage metals: the elements copper, silver, and gold, used to make coins.

coke: a solid substance left after the gases have been extracted from coal.

colloid: a mixture of ultramicroscopic particles dispersed uniformly through a second substance to form a suspension that may be almost like a solution or may set to a jelly (gel). The word comes from the Greek for glue.

colorimeter: an instrument for measuring the light-absorbing power of a substance. The absorption gives an accurate indication of the concentration of some colored solutions.

combustion: a reaction in which an element or compound is oxidized to release energy. Some combustion reactions are slow, such as the combustion of the sugar we eat to provide energy. If the combustion results in a flame, it is called burning. A flame occurs where *gases* combust and release heat and light. At least two gases are therefore required if there is to be a flame. *Example:* the combustion or burning of methane gas (CH_4) in oxygen gas (O_2) produces carbon dioxide (CO_2)

and water (H_2O) and gives out heat and light. Some combustion reactions produce light and heat but do not produce flames. *Example:* the combustion of carbon in oxygen produces an intense red-white light but no flame.

combustion spoon: also known as a deflagrating spoon, it consists of a long metal handle with a small cup at the end. Its purpose is to allow the safe introduction of a (usually heated) substance into a filled gas jar, when the reaction is likely to be vigorous. *Example:* the introduction of a heated sodium pellet into a gas jar containing chlorine.

compound: a chemical consisting of two or more elements chemically bonded together. *Example:* Calcium atoms can combine with carbon atoms and oxygen atoms to make calcium carbonate ($CaCO_3$), a compound of all three atoms.

condensation: the formation of a liquid from a gas. This is a change of state, also called a phase change.

condensation nuclei: microscopic particles of dust, salt, and other materials suspended in the air that attract water molecules. The usual result is the formation of water droplets.

condensation polymer: a polymer formed by a chain of reactions in which a water molecule is eliminated as every link of the polymer is formed. *Examples*: polyesters, proteins, nylon.

conduction: (i) the exchange of heat (heat conduction) by contact with another object, or (ii) allowing the flow of electrons (electrical conduction).

conductivity: the ability of a substance to conduct. The conductivity of a solution depends on there being suitable free ions in the solution. A conducting solution is called an electrolyte. *Example:* dilute sulfuric acid.

convection: the exchange of heat energy with the surroundings produced by the flow of a fluid due to being heated or cooled.

corrosion: the oxidation of a metal. Corrosion is often regarded as unwanted and is more generally used to refer to the *slow* decay of a metal resulting from contact with gases and liquids in the environment. *Example:* Rust is the corrosion of iron.

corrosive: causing corrosion. *Example:* Sodium hydroxide (NaOH).

covalent bond: this is the most common form of strong chemical bonding and occurs when two atoms *share* electrons. *Example:* oxygen (O_2)

cracking: breaking down complex molecules into simpler compounds, as in oil refining.

crucible: a small bowl with a lip, made of heat-resistant white glazed ceramic. It is used for heating substances using a Bunsen flame.

crude oil: a chemical mixture of petroleum liquids. Crude oil forms the raw material for an oil refinery.

crystal: a substance that has grown freely so that it can develop external faces. Compare with crystalline, where the atoms are not free to form individual crystals, and amorphous, where the atoms are arranged irregularly.

crystalline: a solid in which the atoms, ions, or molecules are organized into an orderly pattern without distinct crystal faces. *Examples*: copper(II) sulfate, sodium chloride. Compare amorphous.

crystallization: the process in which a solute comes out of solution slowly and forms crystals. *See:* water of crystallization.

crystal systems: seven patterns or systems into which all crystals can be grouped: cubic, hexagonal, rhombohedral, tetragonal, orthorhombic, monoclinic, and triclinic.

cubic crystal system: groupings of crystals that look like cubes.

current: an electric current is produced by a flow of electrons through a conducting solid or ions through a conducting liquid. The rate of supply of this charge is measured in amperes (A).

decay (radioactive decay): the way that a radioactive element changes into another element due to loss of mass through radiation. *Example:* uranium 238 decays with the loss of an alpha particle to form thorium 234.

decomposition: the break down of a substance (for example, by heat or with the aid of a catalyst) into simpler components. In such a chemical reaction only one substance is involved. *Example:* hydrogen peroxide ($H_2O_2(aq)$) into oxygen ($O_2(g)$) and water ($H_2O(l)$).

decrepitation: when, as part of the decomposition of a substance, cracking sounds are also produced. *Example:* heating of lead nitrate ($Pb(NO_3)_2$).

dehydration: the removal of water from a substance by heating it, placing it in a dry atmosphere, or using a drying (dehydrating) reagent such as concentrated sulfuric acid.

density: the mass per unit volume (e.g., g/cc).

desalinization: the removal of all the salts from sea water, by reverse osmosis or heating the water and collecting the distillate. It is a very energy-intensive process.

desiccant: a substance that absorbs water vapor from the air. *Example:* silica gel.

desiccator: a lidded glass bowl containing a shelf. The apparatus is designed to store materials in dry air. A desiccant is placed below the shelf, and the substance to be dried is placed on the shelf. The lid makes a gas-tight joint with the bowl.

destructive distillation: the heating of a material so that it decomposes entirely to release all of its volatile components. Destructive distillation is also known as pyrolysis.

detergent: a chemical based on petroleum that removes dirt.

Devarda's alloy: zinc with a trace of copper that acts as a catalyst for reactions with the zinc.

diaphragm: a semipermeable membrane – a kind of ultrafine mesh filter – that allows only small ions to pass through. It is used in the electrolysis of brine.

diffusion: the slow mixing of one substance with another until the two substances are evenly mixed. Mixing occurs because of differences in concentration within the mixture. Diffusion works rapidly with gases, very slowly with liquids.

diffusion combustion: the form of combustion that occurs when two gases just begin to mix upon ignition. As a result, the flame is hollow and yellow in color. *Example:* a candle flame.

dilute acid: an acid whose concentration has been reduced in a large proportion of water.

disinfectant: a chemical that kills bacteria and other microorganisms.

displacement reaction: a reaction that occurs because metals differ in their reactivity. If a more reactive metal is placed in a solution of a less reactive metal compound, a reaction occurs in which the more reactive metal displaces the metal ions in the solution. *Example:* when zinc metal is introduced into a solution of copper(II) sulfate (which thus contains copper ions), zinc goes into solution as zinc ions, while copper is displaced from the solution and forced to precipitate as metallic copper.

dissociate: to break bonds apart. In the case of acids it means to break up forming hydrogen ions. This is an example of ionization. Strong acids dissociate completely. Weak acids are not completely ionized, and a solution of a weak acid has a relatively low concentration of hydrogen ions.

dissolve: to break down a substance in a solution without causing a reaction.

distillation: the process of separating mixtures by condensing the vapors through cooling.

distilled water: distilled water is nearly pure water and is produced by distillation of tap water. Distilled water is used in the laboratory in preference to tap water because the distillation process removes many of the impurities in tap water that may influence the chemical reactions for which the water is used.

Dreschel bottle: a tall bottle with a special stopper designed to allow a gas to pass through a liquid. The stopper contains both inlet and outlet tubes. One tube extends below the surface of the liquid so that the gas has to pass through the liquid before it can escape to the outlet tube.

dropper funnel: a special funnel with a tap to allow the controlled release of a liquid. Also known as a dropping funnel or tap funnel.

drying agent: *See:* dehydrating agent.

dye: a colored substance that will stick to another substance so that both appear colored.

effervesce: to give off bubbles of gas.

effloresce: to lose water and turn to a fine powder on exposure to the air. *Example:* Sodium carbonate on the rim of a reagent bottle stopper.

electrical conductivity: *See:* conductivity

electrical potential: the energy produced by an electrochemical cell and measured by the voltage or electromotive force (emf). *See:* potential difference, electromotive force.

electrochemical cell: a cell consisting of two electrodes and an electrolyte. It can be set up to generate an electric current (usually known as a galvanic cell, an example of which is a battery), or an electric current can be passed through it to produce a chemical reaction (in which case it is called an electrolytic cell and can be used to refine metals or for electroplating).

electrochemical series: the arrangement of substances that are either oxidizing or reducing agents in order of strength as a reagent, for example, with the strong oxidizing agents at the top of the list and the strong reducing agents at the bottom.

electrode: a conductor that forms one terminal of a cell.

electrolysis: an electrical-chemical process that uses an electric current to cause the breakup of a compound and the movement of metal ions in a solution. The process happens in many natural situations (as for example in rusting) and is also commonly used in industry for purifying (refining) metals or for plating metal objects with a fine, even metal coating.

electrolyte: an ionic solution that conducts electricity.

electrolytic cell: *See:* electrochemical cell

electromotive force (emf): the force set up in an electric circuit by a potential difference.

electron: a tiny, negatively charged particle that is part of an atom. The flow of electrons through a solid material such as a wire produces an electric current.

electron configuration: the pattern in which electrons are arranged in shells around the nucleus of an atom. *Example:* chlorine has the configuration 2, 8, 7.

electroplating: depositing a thin layer of a metal onto the surface of another substance using electrolysis.

element: a substance that cannot be decomposed into simpler substance by chemical means. *Examples:* calcium, iron, gold.

emulsion: tiny droplets of one substance dispersed in another. One common oil in water emulsion is called milk. Because the tiny droplets tend to come together, another stabilizing substance is often needed. Soaps and detergents are such agents, wrapping the particles of grease and oil in a stable coat. Photographic film is an example of a solid emulsion.

endothermic reaction: a reaction that takes in heat. *Example:* when ammonium chloride is dissolved in water.

end point: the stage in a titration when the reaction between the titrant (added from a burette) and the titrate (in the flask) is complete. The end point is normally recognized by use of an indicator that has been added to the titrate. In an acid-base reaction this is also called the neutralization point.

enzyme: biological catalysts in the form of proteins in the body that speed up chemical reactions. Every living cell contains hundreds of enzymes that help the processes of life continue.

ester: organic compounds formed by the reaction of an alcohol with an acid and which often have a fruity taste. *Example:* ethyl acetate $(CH_3COOC_2H_5)$.

evaporation: the change of state of a liquid to a gas. Evaporation happens below the boiling point and is used as a method of separating the materials in a solution.

excess, to: if a reactant has been added to another reactant in excess, it has exceeded the amount required to complete the reaction.

exothermic reaction: a reaction that gives out substantial amounts of heat. *Example:* sucrose and concentrated sulfuric acid.

explosive: a substance that, when a shock is applied to it, decomposes very rapidly, releasing a very large amount of heat and creating a large volume of gases as a shock wave.

fat: semisolid, energy-rich compounds derived from plants or animals, made of carbon, hydrogen, and oxygen.

ferment: to break down a substance by microorganisms in the absence of oxygen. *Example:* fermentation of sugar to ethyl alcohol during the production of alcoholic drinks.

filtrate: the liquid that has passed through a filter.

filtration: the separation of a liquid from a solid using a membrane with small holes (i.e. a filter paper).

flame: a mixture of gases undergoing burning. A solid or liquid must produce a gas before it can react with oxygen and burn with a flame.

flammable (also inflammable): able to burn (in air). *Opposite:* nonflammable.

flocculation: the grouping together of small particles in a suspension to form particles large enough to settle out as a precipitate. Flocculation is usually caused by the presence of a flocculating agent. *Example:* calcium ions are the flocculating agent for suspended clay particles.

fluid: able to flow; either a liquid or a gas.

fluorescent: a substance that gives out visible light when struck by invisible waves, such as ultraviolet rays.

flux: a material used to make it easier for a liquid to flow. A flux dissolves metal oxides and so prevents a metal from oxidizing while being heated.

foam: a substance that is sufficiently gelatinous to be able to contain bubbles of gas. The gas bulks up the substance, making it behave as though it were semirigid.

fossil fuels: hydrocarbon compounds that have been formed from buried plant and animal remains. High pressures and temperatures lasting over millions of years are required. *Examples*: The fossil fuels are coal, oil and natural gas.

fraction: a group of similar components of a mixture. *Example:* In the petroleum industry the light fractions of crude oil are those with the smallest molecules, while the medium and heavy fractions have larger molecules.

fractional distillation: the separation of the components of a liquid mixture by heating them to their boiling points.

fractionating column: a glass column designed to allow different fractions to be separated when they boil. In industry it may be called a fractionating tower.

free radical: a very reactive atom or group with a "spare" electron. *Example:* methyl, $CH_3•$.

freezing point: the temperature at which a substance undergoes a phase change from a liquid to a solid. It is the same temperature as the melting point.

fuel: a concentrated form of chemical energy. The main sources of fuels (called fossil fuels because they were formed by geological processes) are coal, crude oil, and natural gas.

fuel rods: the rods of uranium or other radioactive material used as a fuel in nuclear power plants.

fume chamber or fume cupboard: a special laboratory chamber fitted with a protective glass shield and containing a powerful extraction fan to remove toxic fumes.

fuming: an unstable liquid that gives off a gas. Very concentrated acid solutions are often fuming solutions. *Example:* fuming nitric acid.

galvanizing: applying a thin zinc coating to protect another metal.

gamma rays: waves of radiation produced as the nucleus of a radioactive element rearranges itself into a tighter cluster of protons and neutrons. Gamma rays carry enough energy to damage living cells.

gangue: the unwanted material in an ore.

gas/gaseous phase: a form of matter in which the molecules form no definite shape and are free to move about to uniformly fill any vessel they are put in. A gas can easily be compressed into a much smaller volume.

gas syringe: a glass syringe with a graduated cylinder designed to collect and measure small amounts of gases produced during an experiment.

gelatinous precipitate: a precipitate that has a jelly-like appearance. *Example:* iron (III) hydroxide. Because a gelatinous precipitate is mostly water, it is of a similar density to water and will float or lie suspended in the liquid. *See:* granular precipitate.

glass: a transparent silicate without any crystal growth. It has a glassy luster and breaks with a curved fracture. Note that some minerals have all these features and are therefore natural glasses. Household glass is a synthetic silicate.

glucose: the most common of the natural sugars ($C_6H_{12}O_6$). It occurs as the polymer known as cellulose, the fiber in plants. Starch is also a form of glucose.

granular precipitate: a precipitate that has a grainlike appearance. *Example:* lead(II) hydroxide. *See:* gelatinous precipitate.

gravimetric analysis: a quantitative form of analysis in which the mass (weight) of the reactants and products is measured.

group: a vertical column in the Periodic Table. There are eight groups in the table. Their numbers correspond to the number of electrons in the outer shell of the atoms in the group. *Example:* Group 1: member, sodium.

Greenhouse Effect: an increase in the global air temperature as a result of heat released from burning fossil fuels being absorbed by carbon dioxide in the atmosphere.

Greenhouse gas: any of various gases that contribute to the Greenhouse Effect. *Example:* carbon dioxide.

half-life: the time it takes for the radiation coming from a sample of a radioactive element to decrease by half.

halide: a salt of one of the halogens.

halogen: one of a group of elements including chlorine, bromine, iodine, and fluorine in Group 7 of the Periodic Table.

heat: the energy that is transferred when a substance is at a different temperature than its surroundings. *See:* endothermic and exothermic reactions.

heat capacity: the ratio of the heat supplied to a substance compared to the rise in temperature that is produced.

heat of combustion: the amount of heat given off by a mole of a substance during combustion. This heat is a property of the substance and is the same no matter what kind of combustion is involved. *Example:* heat of combustion of carbon is 94.05 kcal (✕ 4.18 = 393.1 kJ).

hydrate: a solid compound in crystalline form that contains water molecules. Hydrates commonly form when a solution of a soluble salt is evaporated. The water that forms part of a hydrate crystal is known as the "water of crystallization." It can usually be removed by heating, leaving an anhydrous salt.

hydration: the process of absorption of water by a substance. In some cases hydration makes the substance change color; in many other cases there is no color change, simply a change in volume. *Example:* dark blue hydrated copper(II) sulfate ($CuSO_4 \bullet 5H_2O$) can be heated to produce white anhydrous copper(II) sulfate ($CuSO_4$).

hydride: a compound containing just hydrogen and another element, most often a metal. *Examples:* water (H_2O), methane (CH_4) and phosphine (PH_3).

hydrous: hydrated with water. *See:* anhydrous.

hydrocarbon: a compound in which only hydrogen and carbon atoms are present. Most fuels are hydrocarbons, as is the simple plastic polyethylene. *Example:* methane CH_4.

hydrogen bond: a type of attractive force that holds one molecule to another. It is one of the weaker forms of intermolecular attractive force. *Example:* hydrogen bonds occur in water.

ignition temperature: the temperature at which a substance begins to burn.

immiscible: will not mix with another substance. e.g., oil and water.

incandescent: glowing or shining with heat. *Example:* tungsten filament in an incandescent light bulb.

incomplete combustion: combustion in which only some of the reactant or reactants combust, or the products are not those that would be obtained if all the reactions went to completion. It is uncommon for combustion to be complete, and incomplete combustion is more frequent. *Example:* incomplete combustion of carbon in oxygen produces carbon monoxide and not carbon dioxide.

indicator (acid-base indicator): a substance or mixture of substances used to test the acidity or alkalinity of a substance. An indicator changes color depending on the acidity of the solution being tested. Many indicators are complicated organic substances. Some indicators used in the laboratory include Universal Indicator, litmus, phenolphthalein, methyl orange and bromothymol. *See:* Universal Indicator.

induction period: the time taken for a reaction to reach ignition temperature. During this period no apparent reaction occurs; then the materials appear to undergo spontaneous combustion.

inert: unreactive.

inhibitor: a substance that prevents a reaction from occurring.

inorganic substance: a substance that does not contain carbon and hydrogen. Examples: NaCl, $CaCO_3$.

insoluble: a substance that will not dissolve.

ion: an atom, or group of atoms, that has gained or lost one or more

electrons and so developed an electrical charge. Ions behave differently than electrically neutral atoms and molecules. They can move in an electric field, and they can also bind strongly to solvent molecules such as water. Positively charged ions are called cations; negatively charged ions are called anions. Ions can carry an electrical current through solutions.

ionic bond: the form of bonding that occurs between two ions when the ions have opposite charges. *Example:* sodium cations bond with chloride anions to form common salt (NaCl) when a salty solution is evaporated. Ionic bonds are strong bonds except in the presence of a solvent. *See:* bond.

ionic compound: a compound that consists of ions. *Example:* NaCl.

ionize: to break up neutral molecules into oppositely charged ions or to convert atoms into ions by the loss of electrons.

ionization: a process that creates ions.

isotope: an atom that has the same number of protons in its nucleus, but which has a different mass. *Example:* carbon 12 and carbon 14.

Kipp's apparatus: a piece of glassware consisting of three chambers, designed to provide a continuous and regulated production of gas by bringing the reactants into contact in a controlled way.

lanthanide series or lanthanide metals: a series of 15 similar metallic elements between lanthanum and lutetium. They are transition metals and are also called rare earths.

latent heat: the amount of heat that is absorbed or released during the process of changing state between gas, liquid, or solid. For example, heat is absorbed when a substance melts, and it is released again when the substance solidifies.

lattice: a regular arrangement of atoms, ions, or molecules in a crystalline solid.

leaching: the extraction of a substance by percolating a solvent through a material. *Example:* when water flows through an ore, some of the heavy metals in it may be leached out causing environmental pollution.

Liebig condenser: a piece of glassware consisting of a sloping, water-cooled tube. The design allows a volatile material to be condensed and collected.

liquefaction: to make something liquid.

liquid/liquid phase: a form of matter that has a fixed volume but no fixed shape.

lime (quicklime): calcium oxide (CaO). A white, caustic solid manufactured by heating limestone and used for making mortar, fertilizer, or bleach.

limewater: an aqueous solution of calcium hydroxide used especially to detect the presence of carbon dioxide.

litmus: an indicator obtained from lichens. Used as a solution or impregnated into paper (litmus paper) that is dampened before use. Litmus turns red under acid conditions and purple in alkaline conditions. Litmus is a crude indicator when compared with Universal Indicator.

load (electronics): an impedance or circuit that receives or develops the output of a cell or other power supply.

luster: the shininess of a substance.

malleable: able to be pressed or hammered into shape.

manometer: a device for measuring gas pressure. A simple manometer is made by partly filling a U-shaped rubber tube with water and connecting one end to the source of gas whose pressure is to be measured. The pressure is always relative to atmospheric pressure.

mass: the amount of matter in an object. In everyday use the word weight is often used (somewhat incorrectly) to mean mass.

matter: anything that has mass and takes up space.

melting point: the temperature at which a substance changes state from a solid phase to a liquid phase. It is the same as freezing point.

membrane: a thin flexible sheet. A semipermeable membrane has microscopic holes of a size that will selectively allow some ions and molecules to pass through but hold others back. It thus acts as a kind of filter. *Example:* a membrane used for osmosis.

meniscus: the curved surface of a liquid that forms in a small-bore or capillary tube. The meniscus is convex (bulges upward) for mercury and is concave (sags downward) for water.

metal: a class of elements that is a good conductor of electricity and heat, has a metallic luster, is malleable and ductile, forms cations, and has oxides that are bases. Metals are formed as cations held together by a sea of electrons. A metal may also be an alloy of these elements. *Example:* sodium, calcium, gold. *See:* alloy, metalloid, nonmetal.

metallic bonding: cations reside in a "sea" of mobile electrons. It allows metals to be good conductors and means that they are not brittle. *See:* bonding.

metallic luster: *See:* luster.

metalloid: a class of elements intermediate in properties between metals and nonmetals. Metalloids are also called semimetals or semiconductors. *Example:* silicon, germanium, antimony. *See:* metal, nonmetal, semiconductor.

micronutrient: an element that the body requires in small amounts. Another term is trace element.

mineral: a solid substance made of just one element or compound. *Example:* calcite is a mineral because it consists only of calcium carbonate; halite is a mineral because it contains only sodium chloride.

mineral acid: an acid that does not contain carbon and which attacks minerals. Hydrochloric, sulfuric, and nitric acids are the main mineral acids.

miscible: capable of being mixed.

mixing combustion: the form of combustion that occurs when two gases thoroughly mix before they ignite and so produce almost complete combustion. *Example:* when a Bunsen flame is blue.

mixture: a material that can be separated into two or more substances using physical means. *Example:* a mixture of copper(II) sulfate and cadmium sulfide can be separated by filtration.

molar mass: the mass per mole of atoms of an element. It has the same value and uses the same units as atomic weight. *Example:* molar mass of chlorine is 35.45 g/mol. *See:* atomic weight.

mole: 1 mole is the amount of a substance that contains Avagadro's number (6×10^{23}) of particles. *Example:* 1 mole of carbon-12 weighs exactly 12 g.

molecular mass: *See:* molar mass.

molecular weight: *See:* molar mass.

molecule: a group of two or more atoms held together by chemical bonds. *Example:* O_2.

monoclinic system: a grouping of crystals that look like double-ended chisel blades.

monomer: a small molecule and building block for larger chain molecules or polymers ("mono"

means one, "mer" means part). *Examples:* tetrafluoroethene for teflon, ethene for polyethene.

native element: an element that occurs in an uncombined state. *Examples:* sulfur, gold.

native metal: a pure form of a metal, not combined as a compound. Native metal is more common in poorly reactive elements than in those that are very reactive. *Examples:* copper, gold.

net ionic reaction: the overall, or net, change that occurs in a reaction, seen in terms of ions.

neutralization: the reaction of acids and bases to produce a salt and water. The reaction causes hydrogen from the acid and hydroxide from the base to be changed to water. *Example:* hydrochloric acid reacts with, and neutralizes, sodium hydroxide to form the salt sodium chloride (common salt) and water. The term is more generally used for any reaction in which the pH changes toward 7.0, which is the pH of a neutral solution. *See:* pH.

neutralization point: *See:* end point.

neutron: a particle inside the nucleus of an atom that is neutral and has no charge.

newton (N): the unit of force required to give one kilogram an acceleration of one meter per second every second (1 ms^{-2}).

nitrate: a compound that includes nitrogen and oxygen and contains more oxygen than a nitrite. Nitrate ions have the chemical formula NO_3^-. *Examples:* sodium nitrate $NaNO_3$ and lead nitrate $Pb(NO_3)_2$.

nitrite: a compound that includes nitrogen and oxygen and contains less oxygen than a nitrate. Nitrite ions have the chemical formula NO_2^-. *Example:* sodium nitrite $NaNO_2$.

noble gases: the members of Group 8 of the Periodic Table: helium, neon, argon, krypton, xenon, radon. These gases are almost entirely unreactive.

noble metals: silver, gold, platinum, and mercury. These are the least reactive metals.

noncombustible: a substance that will not combust or burn. *Example:* carbon dioxide.

nonmetal: a brittle substance that does not conduct electricity. *Examples:* sulfur, phosphorus, all gases. *See:* metal, metalloid.

normal salt: salts that do not contain a hydroxide (OH^-) ion, which would make them basic salts, or a hydrogen ion, which would make them acid salts. *Example:* sodium chloride (NaCl).

nucleus: the small, positively charged particle at the center of an atom. The nucleus is responsible for most of the mass of an atom.

opaque: a substance that will not transmit light so that it is impossible to see through it. Most solids are opaque.

ore: a rock containing enough of a useful substance to make mining it worthwhile. *Example:* bauxite, aluminum ore.

organic acid: an acid containing carbon and hydrogen. *Example:* methanoic (formic) acid (HCOOH).

organic chemistry: the study of organic compounds.

organic compound (organic substance; organic material): a compound (or substance) that contains carbon and usually hydrogen. (The carbonates are usually excluded.) *Examples:* methane (CH_4), chloromethane (CH_3Cl), ethene (C_2H_4), ethanol (C_2H_5OH), ethanoic acid (C_2H_3OOH) etc.

organic solvent: an organic substance that will dissolve other substances. *Example:* carbon tetrachloride (CCl_4).

osmosis: a process whereby molecules of a liquid solvent move through a semipermeable membrane from a region of low concentration of a solute to a region with a high concentration of a solute.

oxidation-reduction reaction (redox reaction): reaction in which oxidation and reduction occurs; a reaction in which electrons are transferred. *Example:* copper and oxygen react to produce copper(II) oxide. The copper is oxidized, and oxygen is reduced.

oxidation: combination with oxygen and a reaction in which an atom, ion, or molecule loses electrons to an oxidizing agent. (Note that an oxidizing agent does not have to contain oxygen.) The opposite of oxidation is reduction. *See:* reduction.

oxidation number (oxidation state): the effective charge on an atom in a compound. An increase in oxidation number corresponds to oxidation, and a decrease to reduction. Shown in Roman numerals. *Example:* manganate(IV).

oxidation state: *See:* oxidation number.

oxide: a compound that includes oxygen and one other element. *Example:* copper oxide (CuO).

oxidize: to combine with or gain oxygen or to react such that an atom, ion, or molecule loses electrons to an oxidizing agent.

oxidizing agent: a substance that removes electrons from another substance being oxidized (and therefore is itself reduced) in a redox reaction. *Example:* chlorine (Cl_2).

ozone: a form of oxygen whose molecules contain three atoms of oxygen. Ozone is regarded as a beneficial gas when high in the atmosphere because it blocks ultraviolet rays. It is a harmful gas when breathed in, so low-level ozone that is produced as part of city smog is regarded as a form of pollution. The ozone layer is the uppermost part of the stratosphere.

partial pressure: the pressure a gas in a mixture would exert if it alone occupied a flask. *Example:* oxygen makes up about a fifth of the atmosphere. Its partial pressure is therefore about a fifth of normal atmospheric pressure.

pascal: the unit of pressure, equal to one newton per square meter of surface. *See:* newton.

patina: a surface coating that develops on metals and protects them from further corrosion. *Example:* the green coating on copper carbonate that forms on copper statues.

percolate: to move slowly through the pores of a rock.

period: a row in the Periodic Table.

Periodic Table: a chart organizing elements by atomic number and chemical properties into groups and periods.

pestle and mortar: a pestle is a ceramic rod with a rounded end; a mortar is a ceramic dish. Pestle and mortar are used together to pound or grind solids into fine powders.

Petri dish: a shallow glass or plastic dish with a lid.

petroleum: a natural mixture of a range of gases, liquids, and solids derived from the decomposed remains of plants and animals.

pH: a measure of the hydrogen ion concentration in a liquid. Neutral is pH 7.0; numbers greater than this are alkaline; smaller numbers are acidic. *See:* neutralization, acid, base.

pH meter: a device that accurately measures the pH of a solution. A

pH meter is a voltmeter that measures the electric potential difference between two electrodes (which are attached to the meter through a probe) when they are submerged in a solution. The readings are shown on a dial or digital display.

phase: a particular state of matter. A substance may exist as a solid, liquid, or gas and may change between these phases with addition or removal of energy. *Examples:* ice, liquid, and vapor are the three phases of water. Ice undergoes a phase change to water when heat energy is added.

phosphor: any material that glows when energized by ultraviolet or electron beams such as in fluorescent tubes and cathode ray tubes. Phosphors, such as phosphorus, emit light after the source of excitation is cut off. This is why they glow in the dark. By contrast, fluorescors, such as fluorite, only emit light while they are being excited by ultraviolet light or an electron beam.

photochemical smog: photochemical reactions are caused by the energy of sunlight. Photochemical smog is a mixture of tiny particles and a brown haze caused by the reaction of colorless nitric oxide from vehicle exhausts and oxygen of the air to form brown nitrogen dioxide.

photon: a parcel of light energy.

photosynthesis: the process by which plants use the energy of the Sun to make the compounds they need for life. In photosynthesis six molecules of carbon dioxide from the air combine with six molecules of water, forming one molecule of glucose (sugar) and releasing six molecules of oxygen back into the atmosphere.

pipe-clay triangle: a device made from three small pieces of ceramic tube that are wired together in the shape of a triangle. Pipe-clay

triangles are used to support round-bottomed dishes when they are heated in a Bunsen flame.

pipette: a log, slender glass tube used, in conjunction with a pipette filler, to draw up and then transfer accurately measured amounts of liquid.

plastic: (material) a carbon-based substance consisting of long chains (polymers) of simple molecules. The word plastic is commonly restricted to synthetic polymers. *Examples:* polyvinyl chloride, nylon: **(property)** a material is plastic if it can be made to change shape easily. Plastic materials will remain in the new shape. (Compare with elastic, a property whereby a material goes back to its original shape.)

pneumatic trough: a shallow water-filled glass dish used to house a beehive shelf and a gas jar as part of the apparatus for collecting a gas over water.

polar solvent: a solvent in which the atoms have partial electric charges. *Example:* water.

polymer: a compound that is made of long chains by combining molecules (called monomers) as repeating units. ("Poly" means many, "mer" means part.) *Examples:* polytetrafluoroethene or Teflon from tetrafluoroethene, Terylene from terephthalic acid and ethane-1,2-diol (ethylene glycol).

polymerization: a chemical reaction in which large numbers of similar molecules arrange themselves into large molecules, usually long chains. This process usually happens when there is a suitable catalyst present. *Example:* ethene gas reacts to form polyethene in the presence of certain catalysts.

polymorphism: (meaning many shapes) the tendency of some materials to have more than one solid form. *Example:* carbon as diamond, graphite and buckminsterfullerene.

porous: a material containing many small holes or cracks. Quite often the pores are connected, and liquids, such as water or oil, can move through them.

potential difference: a measure of the work that must be done to move an electric charge from one point to the other in a circuit. Potential difference is measured in volts, V. *See:* electrical potential.

precious metal: silver, gold, platinum, iridium and palladium. Each is prized for its rarity.

precipitate: a solid substance formed as a result of a chemical reaction between two liquids or gases. *Example:* iron (III) hydroxide is precipitated when sodium hydroxide solution is added to iron (III) chloride. *See:* gelatinous precipitate, granular precipitate.

preservative: a substance that prevents the natural organic decay processes from occurring. Many substances can be used safely for this purpose, including sulfites and nitrogen gas.

pressure: the force per unit area measured in pascals. *See:* pascal.

product: a substance produced by a chemical reaction. *Example:* when the reactants copper and oxygen react, they produce the product copper oxide.

proton: a positively charged particle in the nucleus of an atom that balances out the charge of the surrounding electrons.

proton number: this is the modern expression for atomic number. *See:* atomic number.

purify: to remove all impurities from a mixture, perhaps by precipitation or filtration.

pyrolysis: chemical decomposition brought about by heat. *Example:* decomposition of lead nitrate. *See:* destructive distillation.

pyrometallurgy: refining a metal from its ore using heat. A blast furnace or smelter is the main equipment used.

quantitative: measurement of the amounts of constituents of a substance, for example, by mass or volume. *See:* gravimetric analysis, volumetric analysis.

radiation: the exchange of energy with the surroundings through the transmission of waves or particles of energy. Radiation is a form of energy transfer that can happen through space; no intervening medium is required (as would be the case for conduction and convection).

radical: an atom, molecule, or ion with at least one unpaired electron. *Example:* nitrogen monoxide (NO).

radioactive: emitting radiation or particles from the nucleus of its atoms.

radioactive decay: a change in a radioactive element due to loss of mass through radiation. For example, uranium decays (changes) to lead.

reactant: a starting material that takes part in and undergoes change during a chemical reaction. *Example:* hydrochloric acid and calcium carbonate are reactants; the reaction produces the products calcium chloride, carbon dioxide, and water.

reaction: the recombination of two substances using parts of each substance to produce new substances. *Example:* the reactants sodium chloride and sulfuric acid react and recombine to form the products sodium sulfate, chlorine, and water.

reactivity: the tendency of a substance to react with other substances. The term is most widely used in comparing the reactivity of metals. Metals are arranged in a reactivity series.

reactivity series: the series of metals organized in order of their reactivity, with the most reactive metals, such as sodium, at the top and the least react metals, such as gold, at the bottom. Hydrogen is usually included in the series for comparative purposes.

reagent: a commonly available substance (reactant) used to create a reaction. Reagents are the chemicals normally kept on chemistry laboratory shelf. Many substances called reagents are most commonly used for test purposes.

redox reaction (oxidation-reduction reaction): a reaction that involves oxidation and reduction; a reactions in which electrons are transferred. *See:* oxidation-reduction.

reducing agent: a substance that gives electrons to another substance being reduced (and therefore itself being oxidized) in a redox reaction. *Example:* hydrogen sulfide (H_2S).

reduction: the removal of oxygen from, or the addition of hydrogen to, a compound. Also a reaction in which an atom, ion, or molecule gains electrons from a reducing agent. (The opposite of reduction is oxidation.)

reduction tube: a boiling tube with a small hole near the closed end. The tube is mounted horizontally, a sample is placed in the tube, and a reducing gas, such as carbon monoxide, is passed through the tube. The oxidized gas escapes through the small hole.

refining: separating a mixture into the simpler substances of which it is made.

reflux distillation system: a form of distillation using a Liebig condenser placed vertically, so that all the vapors created during boiling are condensed back into the liquid rather than escaping. In this way the concentration of all the reactants remains constant.

relative atomic mass: in the past a measure of the mass of an atom on a scale relative to the mass of an atom of hydrogen, where hydrogen is 1. Nowadays a measure of the mass of an atom relative to the mass of one twelfth of an atom of carbon-12. If the relative atomic mass is given as a rounded figure, it is called an approximate relative atomic mass. *Examples:* chlorine 35, calcium 40, gold 197. *See:* atomic mass, atomic weight.

reversible reaction: a reaction in which the products can be transformed back into their original chemical form. *Example:* heated iron reacts with steam to produce iron oxide and hydrogen. If the hydrogen is passed over this heated oxide it forms iron and steam. $3Fe + 4H_2O \rightleftharpoons Fe_3O_4 + 4H_2$.

roast: heating a substance for a long time at a high temperature, as in a furnace.

rust: the product of the corrosion of iron and steel in the presence of air and water.

salt: a compound, often involving a metal, that is the reaction product of an acid and a base, or of two elements. (Note "salt" is also the common word for sodium chloride, common salt, or table salt.) *Example:* sodium chloride (NaCl) and potassium sulfate (K_2SO_4) *See:* acid salt, basic salt, normal salt.

salt bridge: a permeable material soaked in a salt solution that allows ions to be transferred from one container to another. The salt solution remains unchanged during this transfer. *Example:* sodium sulfate used as a salt bridge in a galvanic cell.

saponification: a reaction between a fat and a base that produces a soap.

saturated: a state in which a liquid can hold no more of a substance. If any more of the substance is added, it will not dissolve.

saturated hydrocarbon: a hydrocarbon in which the carbon atoms are held with single bonds. *Example:* ethane (C_2H_4).

saturated solution: a solution that holds the maximum possible amount of dissolved material. When saturated, the rate of dissolving solid and that of recrystallization solid are the same, and a condition of equilibrium is reached. The amount of material in solution varies with the temperature; cold solutions can hold less dissolved solid material than hot solutions. Gases are more soluble in cold liquids than hot liquids.

sediment: material that settles out at the bottom of a liquid when it is still. A precipitate is one form of sediment.

semiconductor: a material of intermediate conductivity. Semiconductor devices often use silicon when they are made as part of diodes, transistors, or integrated circuits. Elements intermediate between metals and nonmetals are also sometimes called semiconductors. *Example:* germanium oxide, germanium. *See:* metalloid.

semipermeable membrane: a thin material that acts as a fine sieve or filter, allowing small molecules to pass, but holding large molecules back.

separating column: used in chromatography. A tall glass tube containing a porous disc near the base and filled with a substance (for example, aluminum oxide, which is known as a stationary phase) that can adsorb materials on its surface. When a mixture is passed through the column, fractions are retarded by differing amounts, so that each fraction is washed through the column in sequence.

separating funnel: a pear-shaped glassware funnel designed to permit the separation of immiscible liquids by simply pouring off the more dense liquid while leaving the less dense liquid in the funnel.

series circuit: an electrical circuit in which all of the components are joined end to end in a line.

shell: the term used to describe the imaginary ball-shaped surface outside the nucleus of an atom that would be formed by a set of electrons of similar energy. The outermost shell is known as the valence shell. *Example:* neon has shells containing 2 and 8 electrons.

side-arm boiling tube: a boiling tube with an integral glass pipe near its open end. The side arm is normally used for the entry or exit of a gas.

simple distillation: the distillation of a substance when only one volatile fraction is to be collected. Simple distillation uses a Liebig condenser arranged almost horizontally. When the liquid mixture is heated and vapors are produced, they enter the condenser and then flow away from the flask and can be collected. *Example:* simple distillation of ethanoic acid.

slag: a mixture of substances that are waste products of a furnace. Most slags are composed mainly of silicates.

smelting: roasting a substance in order to extract the metal contained in it.

smog: a mixture of smoke and fog. The term is used to describe city fogs in which there is a large proportion of particulate matter (tiny pieces of carbon from exhausts) and also a high concentration of sulfur and nitrogen gases and probably ozone. *See:* photochemical smog.

smokeless fuel: a fuel that has been subjected to partial pyrolysis so that there is no more loose particulate matter remaining. *Example:* Coke is a smokeless fuel.

solid/solid phase: a rigid form of matter that maintains its shape whatever its container.

solubility: the maximum amount of a substance that can be contained in a solvent.

soluble: readily dissolvable in a solvent.

solute: a substance that has dissolved. *Example:* sodium chloride in water.

solution: a mixture of a liquid (the solvent) and at least one other substance of lesser abundance (the solute). Mixtures can be separated by physical means, for example, by evaporation and cooling. *See:* aqueous solution.

solvent: the main substance in a solution.

spectator ions: the ionic part of a compound that does not play an active part in a reaction. *Example:* when magnesium ribbon is placed in copper(II) sulfate solution the copper is displaced from the solution by the magnesium while the sulfate ion (SO_4^{2-}) plays no part in the reaction and so behaves as a spectator ion.

spectrum: the range of colors that make up visible light (as seen in a rainbow) or across all electromagnetic radiation, arranged in progression according to their wavelength.

spontaneous combustion: the effect of a very reactive material or combination of reactants that suddenly reach their ignition temperature and begin to combust rapidly.

standard temperature and pressure (STP): 0°C at one atmosphere (a pressure that supports a column of mercury 760 mm high). Also given as 0°C at 100 kilopascals. *See:* atmospheric pressure.

state of matter: the physical form of matter. There are three states of matter: liquid, solid, and gaseous.

stationary phase: a name given to a material that is used as a medium for separating a liquid mixture, as in in chromatography.

strong acid: an acid that has completely dissociated (ionized) in water. Mineral acids are strong acids.

sublime/sublimation: the change of a substance from solid to gas, or vice versa, without going through a liquid phase. *Example:* iodine sublimes from a purple solid to a purple gas.

substance: a type of material, including mixtures.

sulfate: a compound that includes sulfur and oxygen and contains more oxygen than a sulfite. Sulfate ions have the chemical formula SO_4^{2-}. *Examples:* calcium sulfate $CaSO_4$ (the main constituent of gypsum) and aluminum sulfate $Al_2(SO_4)_3$ (an alum).

sulfide: a sulfur compound that contains no oxygen. Sulfide ions have the chemical formula S^{2-}. *Example:* hydrogen sulfide (H_2S).

sulfite: a compound that includes sulfur and oxygen but contains less oxygen than a sulfate. Sulfite ions have the chemical formula SO_3^{2-}. *Example:* sodium sulfite Na_2SO_3.

supercooling: the ability of some substances to cool below their normal freezing point. *Example:* sodium thiosulfate.

supersaturated solution: a solution in which the amount of solute is greater than what would normally be expected in a saturated solution. Most solids are more soluble in hot solutions than in cold. If a hot saturated solution is made up, the solution can be rapidly cooled down below its freezing point before it begins to solidify. This is a supersaturated solution.

surface tension: the force that operates on the surface of a liquid and that makes it act as though it were covered with an invisible, elastic film.

suspension: a mist of tiny particles in a liquid.

synthesis: a reaction in which a substance is formed from simpler reactants. *Example:* hydrogen gas and chlorine gas react to sythesize hydrogen chloride gas. The term can also be applied to polymerization of organic compounds.

synthetic: does not occur naturally but has to be manufactured. Commonly used in the name "synthetic fiber."

tare: an allowance made for the weight of a container.

tarnish: a coating that develops as a result of the reaction between a metal and substances in the air. The most common form of tarnishing is a very thin transparent oxide coating.

terminal: one of the electrodes of a battery.

test (chemical): a reagent or a procedure used to reveal the presence of another reagent. *Example:* litmus and other indicators are used to test the acidity or alkalinity of a substance.

test tube: A thin glass tube closed at one end and used for chemical tests, etc. The composition and thickness of the glass is such that while it is inert to most chemical reactions, it may not sustain very high temperatures but can usually be heated in a Bunsen flame. *See:* boiling tube.

thermal decomposition: the breakdown of a substance using heat: *See* pyrolysis.

thermoplastic: a plastic that will soften and can repeatedly be molded into shape on heating and will set into the molded shape as it cools.

thermoset: a plastic that will set into a molded shape as it cools, but which cannot be made soft by reheating.

thistle funnel: a narrow tube, expanded at the top into a thistlehead-shaped vessel. It is used as a funnel when introducing small amounts of liquid reactant. When fitted with a tap, it can be used to control the rate of entry of a reactant. *See:* burette.

titration: the analysis of the composition of a substance in a solution by measuring the volume of that solution (the titrant, normally in a burette) needed to react with a given volume of another solution (the titrate, normally placed in a flask). An indicator is often used to signal change. *Example:* neutralization of sodium hydroxide using hydrochloric acid in an acid–base titration. *See:* end point.

toxic: poisonous.

transition metals: the group of metals that belong to the d-block of the Periodic Table. Transition metals commonly have a number of differently colored oxidation states. *Examples:* iron, vanadium.

Universal Indicator: a mixture of indicators commonly used in the laboratory because of its reliability. Used as a solution or impregnated into paper (Indicator paper) that is dampened before use. Universal Indicator changes color from purple in a strongly alkaline solution through green when the solution is neutral to red in strongly acidic solutions. Universal Indicator is more accurate than litmus paper but less accurate than a pH meter.

unsaturated hydrocarbon: a hydrocarbon in which at least one bond is a double or triple bond. Hydrogen atoms can be added to unsaturated compounds to form saturated compounds. *Example:* ethene, C_2H_4 or $CH_2=CH_2$.

vacuum: a container from which air has been removed using a pump.

valency: the number of bonds that an atom can form. *Examples:* calcium has a valency of 2 and bromine a valency of 1

valency shell: the outermost shell of an atom. *See:* shell.

vapor: the gaseous phase of a substance. *See:* gas.

vein: a fissure in rock that has filled with ore or other mineral-bearing rock.

viscous: slow-moving, syrupy. A liquid that has a low viscosity is said to be mobile.

volatile: readily forms a gas.

volatile fraction: the part of a liquid mixture that will readily vaporize under the conditions prevailing during the reaction. *See:* fraction, vapor.

water of crystallization: the water molecules absorbed into the crystalline structure as a liquid changes to a solid. *Example:* hydrated copper(II) sulfate $CuSO_4•5H_2O$. *See:* hydrate.

weak acid and **weak base**: an acid or base that has only partly dissociated (ionized) in water. Most organic acids are weak acids. *See:* organic acid.

weight: the gravitational force on a substance. *See:* mass.

X-rays: a form of very short wave radiation.

MASTER INDEX

21.60

540 C
ChemLab.
Oxidation and Reduction.   V.8.